STEPHEN GETHINS was the Member of Parliament for North East Fife from 2015 to 2019. He was appointed the SNP's Europe Spokesperson when he was elected in 2015. After the 2017 General Election he was appointed Foreign Affairs and Europe spokesperson and led the SNP's Scotland in the World Team at Westminster. Stephen was the first SNP Member of the House of Commons Foreign Affairs Select Committee and he served for two terms. Before his election Stephen worked in democratisation and peace-building overseas including in the Western Balkans and South Caucasus. He also worked in the EU Committee of the Regions and Scotland House in Brussels. Stephen was a Special Adviser to Scotland's First Minister from 2009 to 2013 and focused on energy, climate change, rural affairs, Europe and international affairs. He is currently a Professor of Practice at the School of International Relations at the University of St Andrews. Stephen Gethins is a Trustee of the John Smith Trust, a Special Adviser at Beyond Borders Scotland and the Convener of EU+ME.

Nation to Nation *is a vital contribution to the burgeoning debate surrounding Scottish foreign policy, within or outside the United Kingdom. Stephen Gethins uses his experience and expertise to present a clear-eyed view of where Scotland's interests lie and how best to advance them.* TOM MACLEOD, SKY NEWS

This book is both authentically Scottish and borne of Gethins' own eclectic international experience – a political hinterland stretching from Brussels to Nagorno-Karabakh. Nation to Nation *is a perceptive, highly readable and very timely reflection on the place which Scotland has always had on the world stage, as well as on the role that beckons her in future.* DR ALASDAIR ALLAN MSP (SCOT- LAND'S MINISTER FOR INTERNATIONAL DEVELOPMENT AND EUROPE, 2016–18)

If you are curious about Scotland's role in the world – what it is today and what it could be in the future – then this engaging, informative book is what you need. Full of new ideas, helpful examples, and fun historical details, from an author who knows the ins-and-outs of Scottish foreign policymaking first- hand. DR TAYLOR ST JOHN, SCHOOL OF INTERNATIONAL RELATIONS, UNIVER- SITY OF ST ANDREWS

Stephen Gethins brings deep knowledge, wide experience and sharp insight to the consideration of not just what the current relationship is between Scotland and the rest of the world, but to what it could be if we spoke for ourselves and looked to our ~~~~ ~ e every other normal nation in the world. Debc ̣hat we do to develop it is a key task for the next ̣ ̣om the pandemic and Gethins has kicked

off the debate in a constructive and informed way. MICHAEL RUSSELL MSP, CABINET SECRETARY FOR THE CONSTITUTION, EUROPE AND EXTERNAL AFFAIRS

Just as individual states in the United States pursue their own foreign policy, it is important, and timely, that Scotland begin to articulate its own foreign policy as it seeks to establish itself as an entity committed to justice, rights, and cosmopolitanism. PROFESSOR CARON GENTRY, HEAD OF THE SCHOOL OF INTERNATIONAL RELATIONS, UNIVERSITY OF ST ANDREWS

Luath Press is an independently owned and managed book publishing company based in Scotland, and is not aligned to any political party or grouping.

Nation to Nation

Scotland's Place in the World

STEPHEN GETHINS

Luath Press Limited

EDINBURGH

www.luath.co.uk

*For my wife Anya who has been endlessly patient and
our two Citizens of the World, Mairi and Patrick.*

First published 2021

ISBN: 978-1-910022-09-2

The author's right to be identified as author of this book under the Copyright,
Designs and Patents Act 1988 has been asserted.

This book is made of materials from well-managed, FSC ®-certified forests and
other controlled sources.

Printed and bound by Ashford Colour Press, Gosport

Typeset in 11 point Sabon by Lapiz

Contents

Acknowledgements

IN WRITING THIS book I have relied heavily on speaking to thoughtful people from throughout the UK, Europe and the world. I have drawn from their experiences and observations and am grateful to everyone who took time to share their insights. I was particularly grateful to those who do not share my world view. During a time when political divisions can get far too personal it is worth bearing in mind that most people are able to disagree agreeably. Our society is richer for those differences.

Over the months of lockdown in 2020, I spoke to dozens of people internationally about Scotland's foreign policy footprint and our place in the world. They shared many excellent insights and helped build on conversations I'd had over the past few years. Some of these interviewees support independence; others don't; and some have no opinion on the subject. The same applies to the views expressed about the UK's decision to leave the European Union. Across the board, there was recognition of the need for greater debate and discussion and willingness to think about Scotland's global footprint. Some of the interviewees have been happy to be named, others haven't for entirely understandable reasons. In these days of political polarisation, it is always good to be reminded that there are many thoughtful people with a wide range of views, all of whom are worth listening to. I hope that this will generate and spur further discussion even if is simply to point out the flaws in this book and challenge my own assertions.

This book has been developing in my mind for several years. I am grateful to all of those who have helped me in my journey.

Firstly, my thanks to all of those I have worked with over the years who have helped inform this book. I will always be grateful to Andrew Wilson who gave me my first job. Colleagues such as Duncan Hiscock, Craig Oliphant, Dennis Sammut, Goga Simonishvili, Zviad Mukbaniani, Johanna Petersson, Jonathan Cohen, Anna Matveeva and others who helped me find my way in the NGO community.

In Brussels I was fortunate to work with a fantastic group of committed Europeans such as Micheal O'Conchuir, Helen Frew, Ian Duncan, Kathryn Hallet, Lachie Muir, Pilar Santamaria Gonzalez, Levante Banvalfi, Ian Hudghton, John Edward, Kirsty McVicar, Victoria Bowman as well as the late and much missed Donald MacInnes, Colin Imrie, Eamonn Gallagher and Neil MacCormick.

I am also grateful to my SNP colleagues from Government, Party and Parliament. There are too many to mention but special thanks to Angus Robertson, Alex Salmond, Ian Blackford, John Swinney and Nicola Sturgeon for the opportunities they gave me. To all my Special Adviser colleagues for their camaraderie and commitment as well as the Westminster staff team ably led by Emilie-Louise Purdie with her crucial knowledge of all things Europe. I am perhaps most in debt to the local team who worked so hard including my Head of Office, the irreplaceable Lindsey Alexander, my agent the unflappable Rhuaraidh Fleming, Kirsty Watson, Rhona McLaren, Scott Taylor, Elaine Collier, Callum Riddle, Steven Marwick, Mat Cassen, Henry Orr and constituency convener Moira MacKenzie to name just a few.

I am fortunate to have also worked with some exemplary officials and colleagues from other political parties who have given me some excellent insights. My thanks to my parliamentary colleagues Crispin Blunt, Tom Tugendhat, John Baron, Keir Starmer, Elizabeth Smith, Richard Luce, Alistair Burt, Ann Clwyd, Caroline Lucas and Nick Boles as well as Nick Beech, Ariella Huff and the rest of the Foreign Affairs Committee team.

Over the years I was fortunate to have the input and insights of those who have thought deeply about Scotland's place in the world such as Chrissie Hirst, Malcolm Fleming, John MacDonald, David Pratt, Billy Kay, Stewart MacDonald Jennifer Erickson, Dug Cubie and Patrick Grady. I am particularly grateful to Mark Muller Stuart for his contribution and thought leadership on this issue who has kindly provided the foreword to the book.

I am also grateful to my colleagues at the University of St Andrews who work so hard to make the institution truly, Globally Scottish not least Principal, Sally Mapstone, Senior Vice-Principal Brad MacKay and the Head of the School of International Relations, Caron Gentry. I would also like to thank student Harry Stage for his invaluable research assistance.

Most importantly I am indebted to my family. My parents who brought me up to be aware of the world around me and my wife Anya who has made these past few years possible whilst doing the heavily lifting with two small, wonderful but exhausting children.

Finally, a huge thanks to everyone at Luath Press for their hard work and understanding in helping a first-time author turn an idea for a book into a reality.

Foreword: Mark Muller Stuart

STEPHEN GETHINS' TIMELY book on Scotland's foreign policy footprint could not have arrived at a more opportune moment. With the last-minute signatures still wet on the UK-EU Brexit agreement and Scottish parliamentary elections just months away this new volume of essays on Scotland's relationship with and to the world will surely entice all those who have or share a vital interest in Scotland's future, whether at home and abroad.

For as the UK repatriates certain diplomatic, external and foreign policy powers back to itself from the European Union the obvious question arises as to who and how such powers should be exercised in this post-Brexit world, particularly in respect to Scotland and its relationship with and to the world.

This question is, of course, of no small academic interest. It not only goes to the very heart of the terms and spirit of Scotland's devolved settlement within the United Kingdom but to the future hopes and aspirations, as well as the lives and livelihoods, of millions of Scottish and EU residents, to say nothing of the potential impact on its cultural, educational and economic institutions.

How Scotland sees and positions itself in this post-Brexit environment both within the British Isles and abroad will have critical consequences for the student, worker, business, musician or artist wanting study, work trade or perform abroad.

Gethins' book looks at this critical question from both a historical and contemporary perspective. It not only maps out Scotland's past relationships with Europe, the British Empire and other more obscure parts of the world, it also centres those relationships within the myriad of existing ties of kinship and acts of concord that continue to bind it to these countries and regions.

In doing so, Gethins corrects Boris Johnson's unbounded assertion that there 'are no borders between Scotland and England' to reveal a distinct history of Scotland's own unique international relations with other countries. A set of international relations that not only came to influence the development of its own legal, educational and religious institutions but which also led to a set of separate strategic alliances distinct from those enjoyed by England, many of which still carry resonances to this day.

Such old alliances include ones with vital EU countries such France, Poland and Holland, which Gethins believes stand ready to strengthen their relationship with Scotland whatever the outcome of any possible referendum on independence.

The book is also useful as it charts how a succession of First Ministers of different political hues have, over the last 20 years, not only promoted Scotland economically and culturally within the European Union and elsewhere through the setting up hubs and Scotland Houses but also expressed its commitment towards human rights, respect for the rule of law, climate change and peace-making in its role as a global citizen of the world.

Elsewhere, Gethins uncovers the strong links that have existed between Scotland and the small states of northern Europe – from William Wallaces' early written overtures to the Hanseatic League in the 13th century to the sharing of social democratic, pluralist, rules-based, multilateral, soft power values with countries like Norway and Denmark today, which makes it a credible potential member for the Nordic Council.

More importantly, the book charts out how these values have led to the development of a new civic and inclusive form of nationalism within Scotland. A nationalism that is based not on ethnicity but on a sense of belonging to not only Scotland but also a wider sense of European identify – in which national sovereign powers are happily pooled and shared for the greater comparative good rather than jealously and exclusively guarded, irrespectively of the economic and social consequences.

It makes the important point that the Blackstonian conception of national sovereignty that lies at the heart of the Brexit project – and which led George III to lose America after accusing American patriots of sedition for protesting against the English Parliament's unilateral imposition of English taxes on America – is very much an English rather than Scottish concept. It is partly why 62 per cent of people resident in Scotland voted against Brexit have gone on to consistently vote for parties who advocate in favour of remaining in the European Union.

Indeed, it is within this historical and contemporary political context that a majority of people in Scotland now express their support for independence or at the very least a new vote on independence. Whether or not a majority end up voting for independence is in some sense beside the point. What Gethins' book makes abundantly clear is that, whatever happens, people in Scotland want their country to have a greater voice and role in international affairs in order to both promote its interest and articulate and make good on its values.

Such a finding echoes my own experience of Scotland in the world over the last 20 years. As an international human rights advocate and mediator of conflicts for both the UN and other international organisations, I have seen the role that small nations like Scotland can play in supporting the multi-lateral, rules-based order particularly in the field of climate change, human rights protection, support for the rule of law and the amelioration of conflict through the promotion of mutual understanding between nations and cultures.

I have been constantly struck by how emerging leaders, from around the world, have embraced Scotland as a small but vibrant, soft power nation with an extraordinary historical brand and important constitutional journey to tell. Its strong and separate identity appears to exercise a powerful hold over the world's collective imagination. Whether deserved or not, Scotland is perceived as a proud, independent, small nation which has managed to preserve its distinct culture and identity, despite the presence of a much more powerful neighbour.

This gives it a particular traction with other small nations and groups not only in the European Union, but also with those embarking on a political transition of their own. Its devolved settlement, including within the context of the EU, constitutes one of the best examples of how a smaller nation within a larger state can transition towards greater democratic autonomy in a peaceful and consensual manner, without a bullet being fired.

Since 1998, I have worked in a myriad of conflict situations such as in Turkey, Iraq, Sri Lanka, Libya, Syria, Ukraine, Zimbabwe, Spain and the Caucasus. All of these conflict situations featured issues that touched upon the issue of autonomy and the devolution of power, and virtually all of the conflict parties I talked to became fascinated by Scotland's political journey and referendum process.

That is partly why in 2010 I established Beyond Borders Scotland with the help of patrons across the political divide. Apart from its cultural festivals promoting international cultural exchange it has hosted numerous international delegations who have come to Scotland to either learn lessons about its constitutional journey or to use it as a safe space in which to engage in dialogue to explore their own journeys. These delegations and groups have often been aided by a range of Scottish elder statesmen and women who have experience not just of government but of multilateral diplomacy within the EU, NATO and the UN Security Council at the highest level. Scotland then, is not wanting for expertise as to how to conduct itself within the highest diplomatic forums.

This capacity, together with its world class cultural festivals, universities, research centres and legal institutions, gives Scotland a commanding platform from which to promote its interests as well as peace and mutual understanding between nations, groups and cultures. It is why Beyond Borders, with the help of the Scottish Government, has been able to help over 250 women peacemakers promote peacemaking across the world through its innovative 1325 Women in Conflict Peacemaking Fellowship Programme, aided by the expertise of the United Nations. It is but one of growing set of examples as to how Scotland can and should allow itself to play a greater role in international affairs.

Gethins notes these and other similar developments in his book. He also explores some of the other assets that Scotland can deploy to advance its interests and values around the world, beyond its world famous educational, cultural festival and sporting institutions, such as the potential power of its diaspora. Yet, he is also careful not to be starry-eyed about Scotland's history or the political issues it now confronts. He is not shy to recognise some of Scotland's darker connections to the history of slavery and imperial domination or how others seek to portray his own cause as being 'separatist' rather than 'internationalist' and co-operative in nature.

This book tries to debunk that myth through its examination of Scotland's international footprint. It places Scotland's desire to have a greater say in international affairs as part of a natural political development based around its history and the emergence of a post-imperial set of northern European-orientated social and political values. Whether that voice is to be expressed through a separate sovereign state or within the context of a reformed, devolved, new post-Brexit political arrangement within the UK remains up for grabs – but two matters now appear beyond doubt.

Firstly, people in Scotland are no longer content to let other non-devolved institutions speak exclusively on their behalf or to be promoted and represented merely through their sporting and Walter Scott type heritage. In a recent interview Douglas Alexander, the former Labour minister, described how devolution was essentially an experiment in 'social justice'. I believe the people of Scotland have moved on from that more limited vision.

Secondly, both Scotland and the world around it has transformed since the UK first joined the EU and pooled its diplomatic, external and foreign policy powers with it. It is surely beyond contention that as it leaves the European Union the UK cannot simply return to the status quo ante. The devolution settlement cannot be undone. Powers are now being returned to it and with them comes an urgent and vital new debate and dialogue about the future direction of all four nations in the United Kingdom post-Brexit, including in relation to the efficacy of its current foreign policy institutions. It is a debate and dialogue which cannot be ducked, whatever some politicians might have us believe.

Thus, as the four nations of the United Kingdom, and indeed Europe and the wider world begin to digest, process and come to terms with the full implications of the UK leaving the European Union, it ill behoves any policymaker serious about securing Scotland's political future not to recognise it's growing capacity and desire to promote its own interests and values on the international stage, whether that be through a devolved setting or not. For the positive values that underpin Scotland's current civic nationalism, internationalism and humanitarianism can only make it a greater force for good in the world, whatever its constitutional future turns out to be.

That is why Stephen Gethins' book is so timely and important – it sets the scene for one of the most important debates and dialogues that Scotland is likely to face for a generation. He should be applauded for his even-handed inquiry and for placing this important debate within its proper historical and contemporary context.

Introduction

Then let us pray that come it may,
As come it will for a' that,
That Sense and Worth, o'er a' the earth
Shall bear the gree an' a' that.
For a' that, an' a' that,
It's comin yet for a' that,
That Man to Man the warld o'er
Shall brithers be for a' that.

Robert Burns, 'A Man's a Man for A' That'

FOREIGN POLICY IS at the heart of the conversation around Scotland's future. How Scotland manages its relationships with its neighbours and other international partners is more relevant to decision-making today than it has been for centuries. The UK decision to leave the EU coupled with Scotland's vote to remain has brought differing views of our place in the world within these islands into sharp focus. This is a debate that has come and gone through the centuries so now, just as Burns was influenced by our relationship with Europe and the impact of the French Revolution in 'A Man's a Man', once again our relationship with the rest of Europe has forced us to consider our place in the world.

The EU Referendum in June 2016 and the subsequent difficult negotiations with European Member States was the result of Westminster re-establishing the traditional view of the supremacy of parliamentary sovereignty. That is a view that now differs from the 27 remaining members of the EU who are comfortable with the idea of pooling sovereignty in exchange for economic prosperity and sustainable peace.

That EU Referendum decision resulted in years of parliamentary stalemate. There is a consensus in the UK Government that close relations with the EU are incompatible with its ideas of sovereignty even if those ambitions have come at the expense of the economy and damaged relations with our neighbours. Uniquely the UK has under-taken a negotiation with the aim of establishing more trade barriers.

These developments have met with a sense of bewilderment in Scotland. The idea of parliamentary sovereignty is considered a dis-tinctly 'English principle' north of the border.[1] As a consequence, there has been a significant increase in public support for Scotland re-joining the EU as a Member State in its own right.

The Scottish Government is looking at how our external affairs should evolve, as are academics, journalists, business leaders and oth-ers in civic society. Even though foreign policy, our relationships with other sovereign states, is reserved to Westminster, the devolved admin-istration still interacts with the outside world. Devolution has seen a strengthening in our international affairs including increased interac-tion with the European institutions, a greater role internationally on issues like climate change and using the Scottish brand to promote trade and investment. It has also allowed greater engagement with the diaspora, the millions of Scots living overseas.

Independence would strengthen that international engagement even further as Scotland would become a full state actor on the world stage with the rights and responsibilities sovereignty brings. If Scots are serious about independence more thought must go into our international affairs. And if we are not to regain independence, we must decide what our role will be within the Union and where Scotland fits into a post-Brexit UK that has dramatically changed since 2016 with an ambition for 'Global Britain'.

We need a debate on Scotland's foreign policy, and I hope that it is one focused on substance and reality. No one else is going to have that discussion for us. Too often questions of Scotland's place in the world are focused on the travel plans of Ministers. They are blamed for 'skipping town' rather than scrutinised for their policy and diplomatic achievements or failures that are being pursued 'out of town'. At the same time there should be an assessment of what can be achieved. We need to recognise the positive benefits that a strong foreign policy, if delivered correctly, can bring, from trade to educa-tion and increased stability and opportunity.

In researching this book, I spoke to wide range of practitioners and experts such as the Chair of the European Parliament's Foreign Affairs Committee, senior members of the Biden and Obama White House teams, former Conservative Government Ministers and both surviving Labour First Ministers, among others. They all agreed there is a need for a wider ranging conversation about Scotland's global footprint. That reaffirmed a view that I have had for years that Scotland is an international actor but one that often goes unrecognised even at home.

This discussion must not be restricted to politicians and officials since foreign policy is not restricted to inter-governmental relations. Local authorities, universities, businesses, and community groups among others interact with each other across borders. One of the great achievements of the European project was to bring people across Europe closer together as an integral part of the EU's objectives. The EU has made business easier, allowed young people to work and study elsewhere regardless of wealth or family background and made cross-border cultural and economic collaborations more straight forward; and my generation have benefitted from that project.

Ever since I first travelled outside of the UK, I have thought about Scotland's place in the world and our foreign policy. School trips to France involving long bus journeys from Perth were more joyous for us than I suspect the teachers. However, they were a source of interest of the world beyond our borders that continued during my Erasmus year at the University of Antwerp. Even then Scotland's international profile was clear and other students had a distinctive idea of the country, it helped that it was 1996 and *Trainspotting* was about to take the world by storm.

My interest in foreign policy continued throughout my career working overseas including stints in the EU and former Soviet Union as well as in the political arena at Westminster. Over the years I have been fortunate enough to work in countries as diverse as Nepal and Namibia. I have also gained first-hand experience of the cost of war in places like Bosnia-Hercegovina that I first visited at Christmas 1996 and South Ossetia and Nagorno-Karabakh in the South Caucasus meeting combatants and refugees alike.

I spent four fascinating years in Brussels between 2005 and 2009 while the European Union was rocked over debates about the Lisbon Treaty rejected by voters in France and the Netherlands. I made firm friendships and connections that helped as the UK went through an even greater crisis in its relationship with the EU.

In this work, as one of the few MPs to have worked in the EU and the international NGO community, I was able to bring a unique perspective on European and foreign affairs from experiences outside politics. During the Brexit Referendum and subsequent debates, I was struck by the lack of knowledge or interest in how the EU, made up of 28 independent and sovereign Member States actually operated.

As one of only a small handful of parliamentarians to have lived and worked in Brussels, the lack of knowledge or understanding of the EU really struck me. It was also one of the many problems faced by British negotiators in the Brexit process. I spoke to a number of officials frustrated by the failure of Ministers to understand the EU. Former British Ambassador to the EU Ivan Rogers even said that Prime Minister May and her advisers 'didn't know very much about European councils or that much about the EU' ahead of triggering Article 50 to start the withdrawal process.[2]

However, this international experience was especially useful when I was on the Foreign Affairs Select Committee. Parliamentary committees are where MPs consider issues in greater depth and without the partisanship that dominates debate in the House of Commons Chamber. I worked closely with parliamentary colleagues such as Ian Murray, Crispin Blunt, Catherine West, John Baron, Nusrat Ghani, Tom Tugenhadt, Priti Patel, Ann Clwyd, Royston Smith, Chris Bryant and Nadhim Zahawi, among others. I got to know all of them and find out their perspectives, even if we didn't agree on everything.

My frontbench role as an SNP MP for North East Fife was also important in the development of my thoughts on foreign policy. In 2015 the SNP had become the third biggest party in Parliament and gave us access to some of these key committees as well as front bench speaking slots in the House of Commons for every debate. That experience underlined the need for greater debate and discussion from a Scottish perspective, which is not always the same as a British perspective. I raise some of these differences later in this book such as the potential of the Scottish diaspora, our connections with our near neighbours in northern Europe as well as the relationship Scotland has developed with the European Union.

It is evident from my research that I was not alone in my considerations. Philip Rycroft, who has enjoyed a long and distinguished career in the civil service, told me:

> It was clear to me even in my early days in the Scottish Office that Scotland needed to be able to project its interests overseas.

The issue of Scotland's place in the world, also led Mark Muller Stuart who has worked internationally on some of the thorniest global issues, including as a senior UN official, to reflect: 'Surely the time has come to ask how Scotland can play a greater role in international affairs.'[3]

***

Foreign policy is often thought of as the interactions of one sovereign state with another. The *Cambridge Dictionary* defines it as 'the official ways in which a government has decided to deal with other countries'.[4]

It is rarely that simple and straight forward. A sovereign state's foreign policy is defined by a range of actors within that country who interact with other actors across the world. In modern western Europe, the old ideas of state sovereignty have sometimes been cast aside in favour of nations working more closely together especially since the end of the Second World War and the creation of the European Union. Inside these European states, powerful entities, such as those in Germany, Denmark and Belgium, have asserted their interests at an international level as well.

For centuries Scotland has been no exception, pursuing its own foreign policy interests and ambitions. Scotland has influenced the world and in turn been influenced by the world. This is nothing new, the National Bard Robert Burns and the Scotland in which he lived was heavily influenced by global events not least the American and French Revolutions. It inspired work including 'A Man's a Man' and in turn his work has influenced the world along with the ideas of the Enlightenment that spread from Scotland's major cities.

As part of the United Kingdom, Scotland continues to have a significant international footprint and brand. This brand has been exploited by successive Holyrood administrations and even, though to a lesser extent, by Westminster to achieve its own foreign policy objectives. This has been done in seeking to boost trade, attract tourists and win influence in supra-national bodies such as the EU and even the UN. Scottish Ministers have also sought to develop their own bilateral relationships in countries as diverse as Malawi, Japan, the USA and after the EU Referendum in seeking to define a different relationship with other European countries.

In recent years both the increase in support for independence and the re-establishment of a Scottish Parliament have led to a renewed discussion about Scotland's place in the world.

During the first independence referendum campaign, foreign affairs were part of the debate, but less so than other issues. There was little focus on where an independent Scotland might find its place in the international community and how that would be different from its place in the world if Scotland remained part of the UK. Rather attention was on domestic issues such as currency, the economy and pensions for instance.

Scotland's membership of the EU was an important factor with pro-Union campaigners arguing that Scotland was better served being part of the UK, a large and well-established Member State. There was even an argument put forward by some of the 'No' side that an independent Scotland would be barred from joining the EU. The circumstances for any future independence vote changed radically on 23 June 2016 with the majority UK decision to leave the European Union. This result triggered several constitutional crises in the UK including in Scotland and Northern Ireland, where people had voted, overwhelmingly, to remain.

The 2016 EU Referendum crystallised the increasing divergences between London and Edinburgh, which had been there for years, but most especially over how these two parts of the United Kingdom saw themselves in the context world stage. One had embraced a future that was comfortable with multilateral cooperation and the sharing of sovereignty. The other had rejected it and was seeking a more unilateralist global role, out of sync with its neighbours and the rest of Europe.

With another independence referendum likely, and the legacy of the UK's decision to leave the EU set to dominate politics for years to come, how we see ourselves in the world is at the heart of policy discourse. The world will be reshaped by the ongoing coronavirus crisis and the resultant economic shock. This aftermath will be made worse for the UK now sitting outside of the EU and more isolated internationally than it has been for generations.

The UK will emerge from this health crisis and Brexit as a very different state. Certainly, the UK that goes to the polls at the 2024 General Election will be quite distinct from the UK of 2021. The prospectus for independence and the choices that voters in Scotland make in the future will be very different from the decision they faced in 2014.

* * *

During my time working overseas, there was global recognition of Scotland as a nation with its own distinct brand. From farmers and peacekeeping soldiers in the remotest villages of the Caucasus to those holding high office the corridors of power in Brussels Scotland has an international profile. You can have a conversation about Scotland's future with politicians across the divide in some of the world's most intractable conflicts. The world over leaders are aware of Scotland as a nation even if they held no view on its constitutional future.

Back in Scotland I have been able to speak to some of Scotland's leading foreign policy figures over the years about our role in the world representing a range of sectors including Neale Ascherson (journalism), Winnie Ewing (politics), Angus Grossart (business) and Neil MacCormick (academia). That debate has sharpened up since the EU Referendum with a greater understanding of Scotland's distinctive place in the UK. Brexit has changed and will continue to change the backdrop to the debate over Scotland's future at home and overseas. 'The Europeans get it now in a way they didn't before' as one pro-independence and long-term Brussels resident told me.

This book will therefore make regular reference to Brexit, that is inevitable. Since the summer of 2016, like it or not, the UK has irretrievably changed the way that it is perceived by our partners. Some trace this back further than 2016, to the war in Iraq and its aftermath. Many people in the rest of Europe are now taking Scottish independence and our increased international presence seriously as a result.

Internationally Scotland is now an established story. Scottish journalist David Leask said that when he is writing about Scottish independence in a foreign newspaper his story no longer requires the need for an 'explainer' in a side bar or standfirst introduction. Scotland's history and politics is now part of the international repertoire of news. That has certainly been my experience too when discussing the issue with influencers in other countries.

We must be mindful as to how we conduct our debate on foreign policy however, now that the world is paying attention. That said, the world has limited attention, and this goes for Scotland as it does for Brexit. I was reminded by one MP from another European national parliament, who had taken a strong interest in Brexit, to remember that 'we [Europe] have other problems'. He represented a view in several Member State parliaments that the rest of Europe is keen to move on from the negotiations with the UK. Brexit is receiving less and less coverage in the European media and fading in importance to the rest of Europe politically.

As the rest of Europe moves on without us there is little doubt the whole of the UK has been damaged by the process. Chris Deerin of the think tank Reform Scotland told me that Scottish Ministers need to be out there 'selling the Scottish brand' and that 'economics is the number one priority'. He warned that they might get stick, even from him on occasion if he thinks Ministers are getting it wrong, but 'Scotland needs to develop its foreign policy footprint' and, as he and others have said, we need to differentiate ourselves from a disastrous Brexit within or outside of the Union. Independence supporters argue that the Scottish Government should step up and be more involved in foreign policy, acting like it already has responsibility for foreign affairs.

* * *

There is work to be done if Scotland is to take a greater role internationally but it would not be starting from scratch. The groundwork has been laid over centuries. One of Wallace's first acts in the aftermath of the Battle of Stirling Bridge was to write to Scotland's European partners in the Hanseatic League to tell them that the country was again open for business. Throughout history, Scottish monarchs would seek political matches for their children from throughout Europe to enhance diplomatic links.

More recently devolution and the re-establishment of the Scottish Parliament has seen an increase in interest in Scotland's international affairs. I am grateful to both surviving former Labour First Ministers, Henry McLeish and Jack McConnell, who spoke to me about this book. We may have different views about Scotland's future, but no one can deny their commitment to Scotland's role in the world. In our interviews, Jack spoke about challenging outdated perceptions of Scotland from his time in office that persisted not least after the release of *Braveheart* and Henry discussed Scotland's role in the world at the very highest levels and how he used his contacts from his time at Westminster.

More recently the Scottish Government has won praise for its work on issues as diverse as climate justice, helping women peacebuilders from regions affected by conflict and, of course, in its response to Brexit. As one London-based foreign policy observer told me: 'Scotland has been creative' because it doesn't have formal powers over foreign policy.

Scotland has enhanced its profile and soft power clout since the Brexit decision. This has been duly recognised in Brussels, London and Washington and even in the UN. Jonathan Cohen of the peace-building NGO Conciliation Resources, who increasingly sees a role for Scotland as a safe space internationally, said that 'foreign policy is about making others think well of you when you don't have much time together'.

Scotland's global brand continues to be held in high esteem but there has been a reluctance to tap into that resource at a UK level. I have heard frustrations from diplomats in our overseas embassies that we don't make enough of Scotland's foreign policy footprint such as engaging with the diaspora and Scottish soft power. That said I have also heard from those who think that the UK branding should take priority and that Scotland does well out of being part of a bigger entity.

Whatever your view, this is a debate that can no longer be ignored. Scotland has had a foreign policy footprint since earliest times. That has a big impact on our day-to-day lives from trade and the economy to education and opportunities for our citizens. Our place in the world changes depending on domestic and international circumstances. We are now at another turning point in our history and our relationship with international partners. Now is the time to figure out what the next stage of Scotland's story is.

CHAPTER I

Scotland: An International Actor Throughout History

We are the last people on earth, and the last to be free:
our very remoteness in a land known only to
rumour has protected us up till this day.

Calgacus before the Battle of Mons Grapius
(according to Tacitus)

ON 1 JULY 2020 Prime Minister Boris Johnson was facing his weekly slot at Prime Minister's Questions. There was understandably a big focus on the Covid-19 crisis and the actions of government administrations across the UK. In response to a question about whether those crossing the border from high risk parts of England to Scotland the Prime Minister made the remarks that 'there is no such thing as a border between England and Scotland'.[5]

His comments were met with an immediate reaction from historians and lawyers as well as those working in devolved areas of the public sector. He was even criticised the following day in an editorial of the Union-supporting *Times* newspaper:

> By proclaiming that 'there is no such thing as a border between Scotland England' Boris Johnson writes off a fair swathe of Scottish history. Blithely he ignores the 73 miles of Roman wall running from coast to coast; a couple of wars of independence fought over disputed territory; a treaty of Union that defines the divisions between two kingdoms; a separate parliament in Edinburgh; and a memorable occasion when the Westminster government closed the border with Scotland after the theft of the stone of destiny in 1950.

The newspaper even went back 800 years in history referencing the treaty establishing the Anglo-Scottish border:

> The Treaty of York, which was signed in 1237 and ruled that
> Northumberland, Cumberland and Westmorland were sub-
> ject to English sovereignty, formally established the border in
> a form that has remained largely unchanged.[6]

Evidently, there is a clear idea of Scotland and its history regardless of the view that Scots took of the country's constitutional future.

Scotland has a long history and consequently a lengthy record of international engagement and foreign policy development with its neighbours across these islands, Europe and the world. Scotland has played its part in international affairs and continues to do so, that interaction never stands still.

It is instructive to learn from history and if we are to consider Scotland's foreign policy footprint today and how it may evolve in the future it will be important to learn about the past.

* * *

In all recorded history Scotland has had a distinctive international footprint. Professor Mary Beard even tells us in her history of ancient Rome, *SQPR*, that Roman historian Tacitus argued that 'true Roman' virtue was to be found in the 'barbarians' of Scotland and 'not Rome'.[7] To this day Hadrian's Wall, lying just south of the current border is standing testament to that distinctiveness, much more so than the shorter-lived Antonine Wall. There is also a long-established idea of some kind of border stretching from the Solway Firth in the west to the Tyne and Berwick in the east. In his book on the impact of the Scots-Irish people in the USA, former Virginia Senator Jim Webb refers to their development. He believes that, through history, you can watch the border:

> grow and evolve over the centuries, from the first moments
> of its spiritual, collective birth in the crags and hollows just
> north of Hadrian's Wall as the Roman Empire structured a
> very different England to the south.[8]

It has been argued that the Romans, despite having failed to conquer Scotland, had an impact on Scotland's laws, values, education and how Scots see themselves in the world.[9]

Scotland, like other nations, has its own founding myths. The Declaration of Arbroath talks of the origins of the Scots in Scythia. The Scots of Ulster referred to the marriage of the Pharaoh's daughter Scota with a Scythian general who it was said 'refused to pursue the Israelites' when they fled across the Red Sea. Interestingly the word for Scotland and Scythia is the same in ancient Germanic being *Scutten*.[10]

This idea of a founding myth and links to the ancients and the Holy Land was incredibly important to medieval Scots. Rome was said to have been founded by Trojan refugees with Romulus and Remus being ancestors of the Trojan hero Aeneus. Billy Kay's radio programme on the Declaration of Arbroath refers to the English foundation links to Troy and the Scots to Greece.[11] That branding and links to the ancients were important to Scotland when setting out a distinctive identity and making the case for independence in history.

In 1960, David Murray wrote a chapter of his book on *The Scottish Realm* about Scotland being the first nation in Europe:

> the Scots are undoubtedly a nation. They were moreover the first people in all Europe to set themselves apart as a nation. The essential borders of their land have not changed in any degree for a thousand years.[12]

From earliest times the Scots engaged with partners and played a role in international politics. There is even a reference on the Royal Family's website about the diplomacy of early 9th century king, Achaius. The Royal website states that, although the date of the establishment of the Order of the Thistle is unknown, 'legend has it that it was founded in 809 when Achaius made an alliance with Emperor Charlemagne'.[13]

We know for sure that Scotland has had a diplomatic and economic presence in Europe for centuries. In 1192 Pope Celestine III declared that all Scottish sees (areas of a bishop's ecclesiastical jurisdiction), except for Galloway which was the responsibility of the Archbishop of York, should enjoy the status of special daughter of Rome and so were directly answerable to the Holy See. In the years before the Wars of Independence, Scotland was already a fixture in European affairs. Berwick, Perth and Aberdeen traded across the rest of the continent with particularly strong links to Flanders and the Hanseatic League.[14]

The only surviving document we know was definitely written by William Wallace is the letter of Lübeck (in Germany). It was sent in

October 1297 in the aftermath of the battle of Stirling Bridge that took place the month before. The letter's message to the Hanseatic League, the EU of the day, was that Scotland was once again open for business. It is perhaps fitting and unsurprising that Wallace's only surviving letter is diplomatic and focused on trade with our European partners.

The Wars of Independence had started over the question of succession to Scotland's throne. Alexander III had been pre-deceased by his children leaving the crown to the three-year-old Maid of Norway whose parents were Alexander's daughter and King Erik II of Norway. Margaret died on the way back to Scotland aged just seven on her way to marry Edward of England (later Edward II of Bannockburn fame).

That marriage of Scotland's Queen, whose father had been a Norwegian monarch, exemplifies the diplomacy of the day. Historians David Ditchburn and Alastair MacDonald argue that the 'defining characteristic of Scottish foreign relations was interaction with England'. However, it was not the only interaction or threat. They went on: 'For Scottish Kings there were two potential external threats, one to the west and north, the other to the south.'[15] The Norse had even attacked Aberdeen in 1151, controlled the Northern Isles and had just ceded the Western Isles. Orkney and Shetland were not acquired by Scotland until 1468 and their links to Norway remain strong to this day.

The 'oldest alliance in the world', between Scotland and France, dates from this time. *La Vieille Alliance* was signed by Philip IV of France and John Balliol in 1295 to counter the threat from England. It is even argued that this coalition goes even further back to the alliance between Achaius and Charlemagne to counter a common threat from the Saxons. Over the centuries thousands of Scots have fought in French armies and the links brought benefits to the broader population through common citizenship and trade links.[16] The action did not just take place in France, for example, after the battle of Crécy in 1346, Scots invaded the north of England in support of its 'Auld' ally. It was also in support of the French that the Scots invaded England with disastrous consequences at the Battle of Flodden in 1513 that resulted in the death of King James IV.

It was not just France, however, that represented an important diplomatic relationship to Scotland. In the aftermath of the Battle of

Bannockburn, Scots had to reach out for recognition internationally. Whereas the Scots saw their kingdom as being sovereign, the English Crown perceived the war to be a rebellion against the lawful authorities and William Wallace had been tried and executed as a traitor. Yet, six years after Bannockburn the Declaration of Arbroath, a letter to the Pope, who was in effect the United Nations of that day, sealed international recognition, important even in the 14th century.

The Declaration of Arbroath was also important because Scottish kings derived their power from the people and kings could be removed if they didn't do their job. In Billy Kay's programme the actor Brian Cox describes the document as 'one of the first protestations of democracy'. This is a fact that is recognised internationally given its importance not least in the USA. Tartan Day the day established by the US Senate to recognise the links between Scotland and the USA is marked each year on 6 April, the anniversary of the Declaration. The Senate even recognised what they referred to as Scotland's Declaration of Independence in their own Declaration:

> April 6 has a special significance for all Americans, and especially those Americans of Scottish descent, because the Declaration of Arbroath, the Scottish Declaration of Independence, was signed on April 6, 1320 and the American Declaration of Independence was modelled on that inspirational document.[17]

* * *

Scotland's international connectivity is all around us and part of day-to-day life. I remember at primary school, a new pupil joined us with the surname Fleming. Our teacher explained that he must have Belgian or Dutch ancestry and went onto explain that the name came from Flanders. She told us there had been a big Flemish population in Perth and so he must have had some links. Fleming is a pretty common name in Scotland and reflects the strong trading links that towns up and down the east coast had with Flanders. The Flemish have been described as 'the most important if under-appreciated immigrant groups to have shaped the history of medieval and early modern Scotland.'[18]

The same could go the other way with links to Scotland across Flanders, what is now part of Belgium and the Netherlands. Later in my education I was in Antwerp as an Erasmus student. One day I stumbled across Saint Andries Kirk (St Andrews Church) in the Saint Andries District of the city.[19] Inside the beautiful gothic church is the tomb of sisters Elizabeth Curle and Barbara Mowbray-Curle who had been with Mary Queen of Scots until the end. There is a small portrait of the Queen and underneath the words: 'Mary, Queen of Scotland and France, mother of King James of Great Britain'.

For most people the real connections lay in economic links. The town of Veere in Zeeland, the Netherlands has sought to maintain those links. The town's museum is in the *Schotse Huizen,* 'the Scottish houses', and there is even a local nursery that Billy Kay spotted called *Schotse Schelm* or Scottish rascals.[20] The Scots enjoyed special privileges in the town and kept meticulous records over the centuries. To this day there is a title of 'Honorary Conservator of the Scottish Privileges' a title that was held by former MEP Winnie Ewing who clearly took huge pride in the role. Previously the post was held by the British Consul in Rotterdam after the Scottish community started leaving during the French revolutionary wars.[21]

The depth of trade and size of the Scottish population in the town over the centuries is well-documented. Like any long relationship it was not always a smooth one, with Scots complaining that their food shopping could be more expensive than for the Dutch. The complaints went both ways such as that of one of the town's older Dutch inhabitants:

> who lived next door to the House of the Scottish Nation in 1764 and who wanted to take action against the loud singing and noise made by his Scottish neighbours.[22]

Trade has been central to Scotland's international relations for centuries. Important links were built up and can be found across the length and breadth of Europe, especially with our neighbours in northern Europe. In what is now Poland, the Baltic states, Scandinavia, Russia, Germany, and elsewhere, the presence of Scots and evidence of those who remained can be found.[23] One of the busiest transport junctions in Vienna is called the *Schottentor* or Scottish Gate that used to be part of the city walls dating back to the 13th century and so named after a Scottish abbey that had been nearby.[24]

Even after the Union of the Crowns in 1603 Scots continued to trade independently. When the Scots merchant Robert Jollie was prevented from trading in Hamburg because he was not a member of the English Company of Merchant Adventurers in 1683 the authorities said that rule was not applicable to him because the agreement only pertained to 'subjects of the King of England'.[25]

These links had an impact at home, Professor Steve Murdoch of the University of St Andrews wrote:

> emissaries of Scottish governments and the agents of the opposition contested for the attention of foreign potentates. Their awareness of the importance of international support ensured that many European governments were kept abreast of Scottish affairs. Countless Scots involved themselves abroad in whichever trade or profession they could, regardless of official government policy. They were often to be found in the service of the expanding commercial empires of Spain, Portugal, the Dutch and the English.[26]

The involvement of Scots was not limited to trade, it can also be found in the politics and wars of other countries. We know that Scots were active participants in the Crusades and later, with domestic conflicts such as the wars with Cromwell and the Jacobite rebellions, Scots were exiled and became influential abroad in both politics and the military. Prominent Scots exile James Keith was famed for his military and political service in Russia and Prussia. Professor Murdoch told me that to this day Keith is celebrated as a 'liberator' in Finland where he persuaded the locals that they had been oppressed by the Swedes but were now liberated by the Russians. Steve told me that, to the Finns, 'James Keith is a hero and builds a picture of liberator.'[27]

The dispersal of Scots throughout Europe brought diplomatic clout with traders, admirals and generals across Europe achieving positions of power and influence. Some even sought to influence politics back in Scotland, not least the exiled Jacobites. Scottish soldiers were involved in international conflicts and could be found in royal courts across the continent.

In education there were links between Scottish universities, the rest of Europe and internationally that persist to this day. James IV was tutored by the great scholar Erasmus, who said of his royal student:

> He had wonderful powers of mind, an astonishing knowledge of everything, an unconquerable magnanimity and the most abundant generosity.[28]

Internationalism remains at the heart of our universities who bring in staff and students from around the world. In her installation address in November 2016, Professor Sally Mapstone, the Principal of Scotland's oldest university, St Andrews, remarked:

> We are a university that remains strongly in touch with its Scottish identity, while being profoundly international. Our European identity is a fundamental part of our history as a university... Our founder Henry Wardlaw studied at Paris, Orléans and Avignon before returning to Scotland to set up the University of St Andrews. James Kennedy, the founder of St Salvator's college, studied law at the University of Leuven.[29]

Scotland's links across Europe are bound by shared history, education, trade, emigration and war. The sometimes difficult relationship with England was a driver in Scotland seeking links elsewhere but it was just one part of the equation. As a smaller state Scotland had to rely on building partnerships. This is perhaps one of the reasons that even today Scots can see the benefits of European integration.

Such is the national consensus on the benefits of internationalism that in 1996 the Church of Scotland adopted a report from its Church and Nation committee that referenced the EU and Scotland's heritage:

> Europe is part of our Christian heritage. This is especially true of Scotland where the links are closer than those of England. The Scots are the heirs of a continental Reformed tradition; our church structures are continental rather than Anglican; our law is Roman and continental; our university tradition looks as much to the continent as to the traditions of the ancient English universities.[30]

Given Scotland's historic pro-Europeanism that was considered an uncontroversial statement from the Kirk.

The Catholic Church in Scotland is distinctive from the rest of the UK with recent Popes appointing Scottish cardinals and two successful papal visits to Scotland in 1982 and 2008. Scotland has a long history with the papacy. On the second day of his pontificate in 1878, in what he described as the 'first act of Our Apostolic Ministry', Pope Leo XIII 'gave back to the Scottish people their Ecclesiastical Hierarchy'. Pope Leo had restored the Catholic Hierarchy in Scotland, almost 30 years after the English hierarchy had been restored. The hierarchies had been taken away during the Reformation and Pope Leo highlighted the long history of the Church in Scotland referring to St Ninian bringing Christianity to Scotland 200 years before St Augustine brought it to England.[31]

The history of Scotland was not always easy. Robert the Bruce was ex-communicated by the Pope, Kings of Scotland have found themselves on the 'wrong' side in papal splits and the future Pope Pius II put down the arthritis he suffered in his feet to a mission to Scotland when he was younger trying to get the Scots to attack England during the Hundred Years' War.[32]

Scotland has had to work harder on its international links and is unable to rely upon military might or economic domination over its neighbours. That is a reality that regularly confronts Scottish leaders. According to historians, the Scottish defeat at Humbleton Hill in 1402 made 'the Scottish political leadership come to accept that they could not gain their core diplomatic objective through warfare'.[33]

That posed a diplomatic challenge given some Scots believed its 'international usefulness depended on the military threat which the Scots could pose to the English'. That lesson was not always taken on board as the disaster at Flodden illustrated; historians have argued that James IV thought he 'ought to be involved' in a wider European conflict.[34] It is worth remembering that Scots are not alone in having these historic experiences and memories. This is why the EU remains so important to many small and medium-sized states, they see it as a means of wielding influence and gaining protection from bigger neighbours.

Scots continued to build diplomatic links throughout the 15th century. The marriage of James III of Scotland and Margaret, the daughter of Christian I of the Kalmar Union (made up of Sweden, Denmark and Norway) in 1469 saw the transfer of Orkney and Shetland to Scotland. Thirty years later, in the Treaty of Denmark in 1499, provision was made to recognise and re-confirm the Auld Alliance between France and Scotland and so Scots enjoyed the benefits of common citizenship with them all. It has been argued that these were never overturned in law, which might come in handy in the post-Brexit era for Scots seeking that elusive EU passport.

Scotland's efforts had something of an impact. When the Kalmar Union went through a period of upheaval the Scots backed Sweden in their bid for independence described as 'The Unofficial Alliance' which endured from 1569 to 1654. Scotland was considered diplomatically important enough at that time for Mary Queen of Scots to be considered a worthy wife for the Dauphin and subsequently the King of France. In Norway the 16th and 17th centuries have been referred to as the *Skottetiden* meaning the Scottish period of their history, illustrating the impact the country had at that time.[35]

The Reformation brought major changes to Scotland and how it saw its place in the world and its strategic partnerships. That led to Scotland seeking closer partnerships with other Protestant countries in the North and of course England. At this time, there were concerns of the country's absorption by Catholic France and in the 1560 Treaty of Edinburgh there was agreement by England and France that Scotland should be left to decide its own affairs and French troops withdrawn.[36]

The Union of the Crowns that brought Scotland and England together through a common monarch also changed the way Scotland acted and saw itself. Scotland was still an independent country and recognised as such by European powers even in their courts of law such as the one in Hamburg. The period saw Scots continuing to spread across Europe and beyond, including in Ireland. There was even a 17th century plan to establish a confederal polity bringing together Scotland, Sweden, the Dutch Republic as well as England. Scotland's bigger neighbour to the south was hostile however, and it is argued that it was during these negotiations that 'Scotland lost its place as a significant European power'.[37]

* * *

34

Even with that loss of diplomatic clout Scotland maintained many of its international links and like other European states started the process of colonisation. In 1621 Scotland established a colony in Nova Scotia. This undertaking revealed the challenges of sharing a monarch with another power and that 'an independent [foreign] policy therefore disappeared across the border with James after 1603'. England's interests clearly took primacy including the decision of Charles I to 'return' Nova Scotia to France in 1632 as part of a broader deal.

A few decades later Scotland's political independence came to an end with the Treaty of Union in 1707. A major contributing factor was the Darien adventure where Scotland established a colony in what is now Panama. At its inception, the project was seen as a way of reviving Scotland's economy. But it failed, leaving the country and many citizens, seriously indebted by a project that had sought to connect Atlantic and Pacific trade.

Like many failed foreign policy ventures, it had all seemed like such a good idea at the time. The Company of Scotland, trading to Africa and the Indies was formed in 1695 and five ships, the *Unicorn*, *St Andrew*, *Caledonia*, *Endeavour* and *Dolphin* were seen off from Leith for what they were promised would be a paradise. The enterprise was a disaster in part due to hostility from England, who led diplomatic efforts against the Scots, and from Spain who took military action against the colonists.[38] It was this that in part led to the Treaty of Union.[39]

The dream of linking the Atlantic to the Pacific via what is now Panama was not truly realised until the opening of the canal in August 1914. Even today travelling in the Darien, situated across the border of Panama and Colombia, can be unwise and it remains a difficult area to traverse due to the landscape and thick forests. My brother-in-law Tom Hart Dyke was captured and held hostage in the area in the early 2000s. Upon his release he was told to leave and not come back to their camp on pain of death. After wandering for several days unable to find a road or village he had to take the difficult decision to return, fortunately his captors found pity and helped him and his companion out. He fared better than most of the Scottish colonisers 300 years before. To this day more people have climbed Everest or reached the South Pole than have crossed the Darien gap.[40]

* * *

The Treaty of Union brought an end to Scotland as an independent foreign policy actor but did not end its international influence. The change was not immediate and pan-European politics were at play during the Jacobite rebellions of the 18th century with Spanish marines taking part in the battle of Glen Shiel in 1719 and French troops at Culloden in 1746.

Throughout the 18th, 19th and 20th centuries the Scots played a key role in the British Empire, some might say an outsized role. Scots spread throughout the world bringing their education and business models and establishing Highland Games, Caledonian societies and Burns clubs that persist to this day. It was a St Andrews society that helped set up Princeton and Kings College (later Colombia University) in the USA.[41] A Canadian Member of Parliament reminded me in a conversation that her local Caledonian Society in Toronto was older than Canada itself.

It was not just people who travelled, so too did ideas. The Enlightenment spread far and wide from Scotland and the French philosopher Voltaire is claimed to have commented in 1762, with reference to that thought leadership: 'We look to Scotland for all of our ideas of civilization.' There is debate over the Frenchman's exact remarks but it is clear that the ideas emerging from Scotland were to have a momentous impact across the world.[42]

The Scots had already sought a colonial role when independent and that continued inside the Union. To this day we can see the impact of the British Empire: Scotland now has one of the largest and most widespread diaspora communities anywhere in the world. That has had a profound impact on the rest of the world not least in the USA. There was of course a darker side to the building of Empire. Its impact was felt domestically with the devastating clearances of families and communities. However, we should not be blind to the impact that Scots had elsewhere and the darker elements of our history. Commentator Neil MacKay wrote in an article for *The Herald* in June 2020 that:

> Our ancestors sailed the seas and then they pioneered and
> colonised. Our ancestors wiped out Native Americans to
> make room for farms and cities as they spread out across the

continent. Our ancestors took to slavery like ducks to water.
They ran the plantations, they wielded the whip, they raped
the women, they lynched the men.[43]

If Scotland is to build its international reputation, then one must be big enough to embrace the darker aspects of history. The journalist Alex Massie wrote that Scotland should have a museum to Empire in Glasgow, often referred to as the Empire's second city.[44] It isn't a bad idea.

Nevertheless, like any period of history, Scotland's role and that of Scots in the Empire was never a matter of black and white but rather varying shades of grey. Some Scots benefitted, others did not. The same goes for the scourge of the slave trade. The historian Tom Devine notes that slavery was almost 'universally accepted' and 'almost no one, from intellectuals to politicians and churchmen, had any moral difficulty with the idea of slavery in the 18th century'.[45] Frankie Boyle looks at its impact in his BBC documentary, *Scotland's Shameful Past*, noting all the Jamaica Streets in Scotland joking that it wasn't there because of the thriving reggae scene in Peterhead. In the programme he also looks at the grand architecture in places like Glasgow built on the back of the slave trade.

For a country to build for the future it must embrace its past. Scotland's history has given the country many advantages such as wealth, a diaspora and a well-recognised brand – but that came at a cost. The past should be acknowledged openly and honestly and as a result built upon.

***

In recent years Scotland has once again increased its international engagement. Membership of the EU in the 1970s changed how Scotland saw itself in the world and the way in which the constituent parts of the UK interacted with each other. Those changes have become apparent with Brexit; there had been a failure to grasp that the UK that joined the EU is not the same entity as the one that left. EU membership was embraced by Scotland, even before devolution, changing outlooks, relationships and perceptions of how we engaged within the UK and with our neighbours.

The establishment of the Scottish Parliament was of course important, although there was plenty of work going on previously. Ian

Lang set out a strategy for engaging with the EU in 1990 and the EU Council was held in Edinburgh in 1992 (though this was criticised as involving Scotland simply by having the city as a 'bonnie backdrop'). EU membership also changed the SNP: Winnie Ewing was instrumental in building an acceptance of the EEC (European Economic Community) in the SNP. She became a member of the European Parliament in 1974 and felt much more at home in that institution than she ever did in the House of Commons.[46] Indeed the SNP often sent its most talented parliamentarians to the European Parliament not least the great and much missed Professor Neil MacCormick and Allan Macartney.

These developments did not happen overnight and, just like within the SNP and across Scotland, attitudes to Europe have changed over the years. The EU itself has also changed the ways in which the constituent parts of the UK interacted with one another. Vanessa Glynn, a former EU Director in the Scottish Government, who worked in both the devolved and UK administration, set out the evolution of that relationship to me. It started with her experiences working with the Secretary of State for Scotland:

> Working on Scotland's relationship with the EU over 20 years (1990–2011) – and under governments of all parties – I saw a very clear deepening and expansion in engagement over time. In the early 1990s Secretary of State Ian Lang was keen to demonstrate that Scotland was best served in all things European from behind the UK nameplate, with EU efforts put almost exclusively into structural funds and fishing.

That is similar to Philip Rycroft's recollections when he worked on the establishment of Scotland Europa during Ian Lang's tenure as Secretary of State for Scotland. There was positive engagement to ensure that Scotland's voice was heard in Brussels. The change of government in 1997 and the election of the first Scottish Parliament in 1999 took the relationship to a new level. Vanessa Glynn continued:

> This [relationship] changed with devolution and the establishment of Scotland House in Brussels. Donald Dewar and his Labour successors as First Minister, saw that Scotland needed to engage across a wider range of issues and develop

more direct relationships with the EU institutions and Member States, while always keeping close to UK positions and emphasising Scotland's regional status.

Another change and a different emphasis came in 2007 with the election of the first ever SNP Government at Holyrood. Vanessa Glynn recognised that this brought in a government whose ambition was ultimately Scotland as a full Member State of the EU rather than as a strong 'region' within a Member State:

> The arrival of an SNP administration saw a more ambitious and focused approach to Scotland's EU interests. Alex Salmond put a lot of emphasis on high-quality European relationships. Official visits to, for example, France, Catalonia and Brussels were focused on securing meetings with highest-level political and economic actors possible and direct involvement by him in securing the results he wanted in terms of Scotland's business opportunities and political profile. On EU issues, efforts became more focused on achieving tangible outcomes in terms of wins for Scotland in renewable energy, fisheries, justice and home affairs and research funding. There was also a strong emphasis on exemplary implementation of EU legislation in Scotland and taking advantage of the slight increases in sub-state participation offered by the Lisbon Treaty in terms of subsidiarity.

This is a relationship that continues to evolve. Michael Russell has undertaken two stints as an External Affairs Minister first in 2009 and then from 2018 until his retirement from the Scottish Parliament in May 2021. The biggest change he has seen is that just as attitudes towards Scotland have changed in Europe, the SNP's thinking has become more developed and the Ministerial brief more important as independence is taken increasingly seriously in Brussels and elsewhere.

It was not just our relationship with Europe that changed with devolution. Following Donald Dewar's initiative to open Scotland House in Brussels, Henry McLeish established an office in the UK Embassy in Washington DC and Jack McConnell opened a similar post in Beijing. There were all convinced that they should expand Scotland's international footprint.

McConnell told me of the innovative moves that were made to ensure Scotland could spend money in support of the international development policy he established. They used the flexibility in the Scotland Act which allowed the devolved government to spend funds in support of the work of the UK Government in reserved areas. He also referred to the way in which, from China to Malawi, as a national leader in a sub-state government he was able to have more open and relaxed relationships with leading political figures in other countries.

Henry McLeish was also keenly involved in developing Scotland's international relationships. The former First Minister talks of the importance of the 40–50 strong Scottish caucus in the United States Congress. He also had a meeting with President Bush through the Ambassador in Washington DC helped by the Bush family oil connections in Scotland.

More recently both Alex Salmond and Nicola Sturgeon have taken proactive stances on foreign policy. In 2007, for the first time, there was a government in Edinburgh that had a foreign policy that diverged from the party of the British Foreign Secretary with different parties in power at Westminster and Holyrood. Internationally there was a focus on trade and investment with visits to the USA and China among other places.

The SNP have also focused on areas such as peace-building work with the UN, an ambitious climate change agenda and Ministers who regularly talk up the benefits of multilateralism, sharing sovereignty and a clear pro-European outlook. The divergence between UK and Scottish foreign policy is seen in a much more multilateralist approach in Edinburgh and one that sees the benefit of sharing sovereignty through the EU for instance. That is clearly ill at ease with the UK that sees itself as a large, nuclear armed country that can seek its own trade deals outside the commonly established rules that its neighbours abide by in the EU.

* * *

That expansion in international affairs and Scotland's foreign policy footprint has accelerated since the advent of devolution but it is building on an historic legacy. In 1942 Charles de Gaulle travelled to Edinburgh to make the case for France during its darkest hours in the long years of Nazi occupation. There he referred to the 'oldest alliance in the world', dating back centuries. For the French leader, who even told Harold MacMillan his great-grandmother was Scottish, there was also a more personal and recent experience with the sacrifices made by Scottish troops at St Valery-en-Caux where he says their bravery helped him fight on.[47, 48] The emotion in the speech is plain:

> In every combat where for five centuries the destiny of France was at stake, there were always men of Scotland to fight side by side with men of France, and what Frenchmen feel is that no people has ever been more generous than yours with its friendship.[49]

Links between countries can go back centuries making them durable but also fluid. Historic narratives change all the time as do bilateral relations. In 1942 France needed help and de Gaulle was able to draw upon the Auld Alliance and the long-standing links in making his case.

The French were not alone in appealing to their historic links with Scotland during the Second World War. The same went for Poles who were able to draw on historic links between Scotland and Poland at that time as well. The Poles, whose country had seen so much Scottish immigration hundreds of years before, seized upon this connection and 'talked about a relationship that went back hundreds of years and so they should be accepted by the community'. In other words, they were arguing that the Poles and Scots had natural affinity.[50] This helped them gain acceptance in their new home by appealing to a sense that there was a historic relationship between Scotland and Poland. To this day you can still see the impact of those Poles in the defences they built around Fife and the war graves of free Poles in cemeteries across Scotland.

Narratives are shaped by history. Scotland has close links with countries throughout the world forged over centuries by commerce, conflict, migration and education. Those links are present today and are ready to be built upon. Regardless of its constitutional future Scotland is not starting from scratch as it considers the next stage of its foreign policy development. In the aftermath of the Brexit and Covid crises that illicit serious questions about its future within the UK big decisions needs to be made about the country's future.

Our international relationships are moulded in many ways. Thousands of students come to Scotland every year and Scotland's Higher Education sector is very internationalised and respected throughout the world. Culturally, in music, literature and across the arts, there is also a distinction. Perhaps the most celebrated is our National Bard Robert Burns who is revered throughout the world, his poetry translated into many languages. Across the vastness of the former Soviet Union his work is well-known and available in even minority languages such as Ossetian. In the suburbs of Moscow, you can still find his poetry piled on booksellers' carts outside metro stations. The Annual Burns Supper is said to be one of the biggest nights of the year in the Canadian Parliament. There are 60 statues to Burns in the world putting him third behind Queen Victoria and Christopher Columbus in the statue league tables, and he is perhaps the least controversial of the three. Likenesses of Burns are to be found in London, the Sorbonne, Canberra, Montreal and across the USA including a replica of his cottage in Atlanta.[51]

In sport there are also links, Scots having been central to the spread of games like football and rugby. Football is the international language that can be a conversation opener. Working and studying overseas people knew my own team, Dundee United.

Pulitzer Prize winning author James Michener fell in love with the team as a student at St Andrews: 'Dundee United was my kind of team, brash, brawling and brave.'

He would keep up to date with the team's progress in what he called the 'better papers' noting they had been promoted by reading about it in the *New York Times*.[52] The team is known throughout Europe given its record in European club competition.

It has also enjoyed brushes with Hollywood glamour. Neil Paterson, team captain in the 1936–37 season is the only footballer to have won an Oscar for *Room at the Top* denying *Ben Hur* a record-breaking 12th Oscar in the 1960 awards. Grace Kelly even went to a match at Tannadice and was immortalised in the song *Hamish the Goalie* (named after the Dundee United goalkeeper Hamish McAlpine) by Michael Marra, later covered by Leo Sayer. These stories are just of one football team and could be replicated by other football and sports teams across the country.

* * *

Foreign policy through its various means is about building links between people. Diplomats will seek to build connections and make people aware and fond of their country. Shared history, a common appreciation of culture or memories of sports have a role to play in that. Max Hastings reviewed *Soft Power* by Robert Winder for the *Sunday Times*. In his review he wrote, quoting from the book:

> A nation's standing in the world, he [Winder] writes, has in recent times not been measured only by its foreign policy or the size of its fleet: 'In the end it boiled down to something simple: whether a country was liked.'[53]

Scotland may not have a big army or, as the MP for the Western Isles and SNP Group Leader in the 1970s Donnie Stewart once joked, the aim of 'total world domination', but the country is liked.

As we stand at the hinge of history it is important to remember that, as Professor Steve Murdoch put it, 'historic narratives change all the time' along with how countries see themselves in the world.

In 2020, a major Finnish newspaper *Helsingin Sanomat* ran a piece about Scotland, commenting that 'gradually England and Scotland have been drifting apart, almost like tectonic plates'. The newspaper queried whether Scotland with its views on climate change, multilateralism and about the same size as Finland, Norway and Denmark would be better placed aligned with the Nordic states. The author of the piece, Alistair Heather, highlighted the policy commonality to be found in the Nordics, as have others such as writer and broadcaster Lesley Riddoch.[54]

This isn't such a crazy idea with plenty in common and a history of connectivity. Alistair Heather writes: 'Ideas of identity are unfixed, and Scotland's self-image seems increasingly up for grabs.' It is right and he correctly points out that a century ago Finland was very much seen as part of Russia's sphere of influence whereas now it is very much part of the Nordics and EU. The same goes for the Baltics who have transformed their identities in the brief time since they regained their independence from Moscow. Former President of Estonia, Toomas Hendrik Ilves, remarked in response to the question of Scotland's independence that:

For the first 34 years of my life (still more than half), anyone who said my country, Estonia, would ever be free again was considered a nut job. We have been independent again for 30 years, a member of the EU and NATO, and one of the most digitally advanced countries in the world.[55]

It is not restricted to Europe with countries the world over redefining themselves. During the EU Referendum, members of the Foreign Affairs Committee met with the Canadian, Australian and New Zealand Ambassadors in Brussels. The message was clear that, although none of those Commonwealth countries took an official position, the consensus was that it was better for them if the UK remained in the EU. All saw the benefits of the single market and although the Commonwealth was important, they were clear that they were no replacement. This came as something of a shock to some Brexiteers realising that all these countries looked, instead of to the UK, to their neighbours and had been busy developing links with Asia, the Pacific and other strategic partners. The ties of Empire were there but clearly not as important in the 21st century as they perhaps had been in the 19th or 20th centuries.

Our place in the world is by no means set in stone and history shows us that it evolves and changes. Regardless of our constitutional future now is the time for us to reflect on history and what happens next. Scotland is better placed than most countries in the world to meet those challenges with a strong brand and links throughout the world.

CHAPTER 2

Scotland's Diaspora: 'You're In!'

A large part of the world turns out to be 'Scottish' without even knowing it.

Arthur Herman, *How the Scots Invented the Modern World*

THE ROAD FROM Yerevan, the capital of Armenia, to Stepanakert, the capital of the disputed territory of Nagorno-Karabakh, across the Laçin corridor is one of the most beautiful in a region blessed with outstanding scenery. Back in 2002 I travelled across that road with two ex-combatants from the conflict that had broken out between Armenians and Azerbaijanis as the Soviet Union collapsed about 15 years earlier.

What was most striking about the road was its quality and lack of potholes. At that time travelling anywhere in the South Caucasus by car meant a gruelling trip over miles of pothole-littered roads. Yet the road over some of the most remote and beautiful areas was the best road I travelled on in the region and certainly, at that time, better than the main road between Tbilisi and Yerevan.

The reason for the investment was the road's political importance linking the two capitals of Armenia and Nagorno-Karabakh.. Yet it had not been entirely funded by the government and every so often a sign would pop up along the side of the road marking the contribution of the diaspora groups who had provided funding for the lifeline route.

15 years later the dispute was in the news again when fighting broke out in the area with Azerbaijan pushing back ethnic Armenian troops from parts of the disputed region in the Autumn of 2020.

The same, now more worn, road provided one of the escape routes for ethnic Armenian refugees fleeing advancing Azerbaijani troops.

For years the diaspora has provided political and financial support to Armenia and the authorities in Nagorno-Karabakh. It is not alone and, as we shall explore in this chapter, countries throughout the world have powerful diaspora communities that have a big impact on how those countries conduct their international affairs.

Diaspora comes from the Greek 'to scatter about'. Just as the Greeks were 'scattered' throughout the known world centuries ago so too are Scots to be found in every corner of the modern world. Scotland's global diaspora has been estimated to be 40 million.[56] For every Scot to be found in Scotland there are at least another eight claiming a connection somewhere else. It is hard to estimate the size of the diaspora entirely, some think it could be as big as 70 million and even 100 million has been mentioned.[57]

There are those who may be unaware that they are a member of a diaspora as well as members who self-define as part of the diaspora even though they may not have any genealogical links such as 'affinity Scots'. The diaspora has grown over the centuries bringing its own challenges and opportunities 'back home'.

Few countries in the world have a diaspora to match that of Scotland in terms of size and influence. History has seen the dispersal of Scots across the world. Countries such as Armenia, Israel and Ireland among others have demonstrated the powerful potential in economic and political terms of a diaspora community. There is no reason why Scotland shouldn't be making more use of its diaspora as part of its foreign policy toolkit.

Our definition of who can be a Scot is rightly broad and inclusive, basically 'if you live here you are one of us'. That approach is also taken to membership of the diaspora community. It is generally considered that the diaspora consists of those with links to Scotland either through ancestry or affinity. Some go even further, the author Arthur Herman starts his best-selling book, *The Scottish Enlightenment: The Scots Invention of the Modern World*, with the words 'I am not a Scot or even of Scottish descent.' He then goes on to write:

> 'being Scottish turns out to be more than just a matter of nationality or even culture. It is also a state of mind, a way of viewing the world and our place in it.'

Herman even goes so far as to state that 'a large part of the world turns out to be "Scottish" without even knowing it.'[58] His attitude is similar to that of Scotland's politicians and enterprise agencies towards the diaspora, to be as inclusive as possible.

That broad definition goes beyond policy. You will find Highland Games and gatherings taking place around the world and I can remember such events being advertised in Belgium, small towns in the Rockies and elsewhere. A recent work on the diaspora by Momentous Change Ltd., a company set up by my former parliamentary colleagues, Roger Mullin and Michelle Thomson, studied the perception of the diaspora. That report quotes a review of a book by David Hesse on the 'affinity Scots' found across Europe.[59] In that review Dr Sean Damer of the University of Edinburgh notes:

> It came as a complete surprise to me to learn from this book that there are more than 20 clan societies, 200 pipe bands and 130 Highland Games in northern Europe, not to mention several dozen societies commemorating and/or re-enacting Scottish history... This Scotomania is widespread in north-western Europe in French, Dutch and German-speaking countries; it's a unique phenomenon. There is no requirement for Scottish ancestry to become a member, one can become an 'affinity Scot'.[60]

Reaching out to 'affinity Scots' is incredibly important, and the broad inclusive definition brings wide ranging benefits. That does however, mean it is difficult to assess the diaspora properly. We should take some pride in the fact that whatever Scotland is selling people are buying into it. That is an important and powerful part of the country's branding and one that has tangible benefits for commerce, education and even diplomacy.

This inclusivity was highlighted by Alex Salmond in a speech to the Brooking Institute in Washington DC in April 2013 when he said:

> And the census recorded that ten million people in these United States have Scots or Scots-Irish ancestry. However, the opinion poll suggested that 30 million people claimed Scots or Scots-Irish ancestry, which, I have to say, I thought was the most fantastic compliment that had been paid to any nation in history. Twenty million people wanted to be

Scottish. And so, one of the messages I've been giving in the
United States is you're in. It's done.

The approach, taken by politicians and government bodies, is to be
as all-embracing as possible. If you have any link to Scotland, think
you have one or just have an affinity that's fine – you are in. As
we will look at later in this chapter, diasporas can bring an added
dimension to foreign policy that delivers significant benefits. Even
the slightest connection will be one that embassies the world over
will seek to exploit.

* * *

Scotland's diaspora and connections are truly global. In every corner
of the world there are links to Scotland and the Scots.

The most obvious of these is of course in the United States. It is
estimated that just ten of 44 the Presidents of the United States have
no connection to Scotland.[61] Donald Trump's mother was of course
a Gaelic speaker from Lewis whose cousins still live on the island.
Even Uncle Sam himself is said to have been based on a butcher, Sam
Wilson, from Greenock.

It is hard to underestimate the impact that the Scots have had
on the USA. There are Scottish societies scattered the length and
breadth of the country. On the homepage of the Chicago Scots,
Scottish American Museum and Hall of Fame it carries the quote
from US President Woodrow Wilson that: 'Every line of strength in
American history is coloured in Scottish blood.'[62]

Former US Senator and author, Jim Webb, wrote about the impact
of the Scots-Irish in America. This is a diaspora he wrote that 'was
formed first and foremost in Scotland' and to understand it one must
transport themselves back 'nearly two thousand years ago, and then
trace a series of events that culminated in the Battle of Bannockburn'.
He writes movingly of his brother playing the bagpipes at his father's
funeral and that 'the Scots-Irish did not merely come to America,
they became America'.

This has even been seized by the Irish as well. On the day of the
opening of a new Honorary Consulate in Charleston, South Carolina
the Irish Consulate in Atlanta noted that the state had 'one of the
highest proportions of Irish and Scots-Irish in the south-east US'.[63]

To some this may seem like pretty romanticised stuff that may provoke eye rolling. However, it is incredibly powerful for those overseas who feel an affinity with Scotland and it is a valuable foreign policy and diplomatic asset. Countries that spend hundreds of millions of pounds a year on building connections in the USA do not even come close to that kind of reach and emotional connection.

The annual Tartan Day celebrations provide an important opportunity for Scottish businesses, universities and others to showcase their country in the world's most powerful country with the biggest economy. That is a long-standing connection and there is even political reach with the Scottish caucus keen to engage with the Scottish Government. The emotional connection is important, and it is good politics for elected representatives to be seen to engage with Scotland given that they will have an important diaspora community in their states and districts. During a conversation with former Scotland Office Minister, Ian Duncan, about this book he pulled out a badge that read 'Scots for Nixon'. He had found it in a shop in New Hampshire and was clearly produced for one of the former President's election campaigns.

The same reach goes beyond the USA and there are similar Scots diasporas across the world. The *Scotland.org* website run by the Scottish Government provides an insight into some of these links.[64] Canada has clear Scottish connections since Scotland set up its first settlements there. The website goes back further and even uses the claims that the first Scottish links can be traced back to over a thousand years ago when the Vikings landed in Newfoundland.

Today five million Canadians, out of a population of 38 million, claim Scottish descent. Fourteen Canadian Prime Ministers can claim Scottish ancestry including the current incumbent and Canada's 23rd Prime Minister, Justin Trudeau. Across the country there are strong cultural, educational, economic and family links that have persisted, and the country also celebrates Tartan Day. On 25 January 2021 Burns Night was even marked in Parliament with MP Kirsty Duncan telling the Chamber that 'today Canadians of Scottish heritage celebrate the memory and legacy of poet Robert Burns' in her remarks noting the importance of Robert Burns to Canadians.[65]

The same goes elsewhere in the world and the Commonwealth where strong Scottish links are to be found. In Australia 10 per cent of the population have Scottish roots. Even in the most Australian of sports, the first game of Aussie rules football took place between Melbourne Grammar and Scotch College. Australian rockers AC/DC were formed by Scots emigrants, you can even visit singer, Bon Scott's statue in his hometown of Kirriemuir, Angus.

In 2014 Guy Scott assumed the interim Presidency of Zambia after the death of President Sata. He was the first white African President in the post-apartheid and post-colonial era. He is part of the Scottish diaspora and was born in Livingstone in Zambia, named after another famous Scot. He was said to be very proud of his Scottish roots when he met up with Scottish Government Minister Humza Yousaf and Special Adviser Malcolm Fleming in January 2014. The list could go on and stories of the diaspora have filled many fine books and broadcasts.

Across the world evidence of the impact of Scots is global. There are 34 Aberdeens including Aberdeen Harbour in Hong Kong, the Aberdeen Bazaar in Port Blair in the Andaman and Nicobar Islands in the Indian Ocean and of course Aberdeen in Washington state where Kurt Cobain of Nirvana came from. I grew up in Perth (Scotland) and have lost count of the number of times that I was told 'you don't sound like an Australian' though of course I could have been mistaken as coming from any of the towns called Perth across the world including the one just south of Guyana's capital Georgetown. Towns and cities the world over bear the hallmarks of Scottish settlement and those links remain.

Scots are viewed rather positively throughout the world with a good international branding. That should not mean we are unrealistic about the positive and negative legacies of history. As a nation we should be fully aware of what that has meant for others.

Scots were at the heart of building the British Empire. In his book on the English, Jeremy Paxman quotes Sir Charles Dilke who wrote in 1869:

> In British settlements from Dunedin to Bombay, for every Englishman who has worked himself up to wealth from small beginnings you find ten Scotchmen.

Paxman quotes him further (he says mischievously): 'It is strange indeed that Scotland has not become the popular name for the United Kingdom.'

Neil Ferguson writes in his book *Empire* that in the 1750s 'the East India Company was at the very least half Scottish' even though Scots made up about a tenth of the population of the British Isles at the time.[66]

As we explored in Chapter 1, Scots have a mixed past and one that it is important to embrace and be aware of. There is an opportunity globally because of the impact that Scots have made and continue to make however we must also be honest with ourselves that many of those connections are not entirely benign in their origin.

Connections also go beyond the Commonwealth and the English-speaking world. In South America where football is something akin to a religion there are strong Scottish links to the establishment of the game. This was due to Scots, and others from these islands, building business links across that continent. Author Billy Kay even argues that the South Americans adapted their style of play from Scots, albeit with apparently more long-term success. The Scottish Wanderers played in Brazil and it was a Scot, Joh Harley, who was credited with transforming the game in Uruguay just 20 years before they won the first world cup.[67]

Across the River Plate in Argentina the impact was perhaps even more profound. Alexander Watson Hutton is described as 'the father of Argentinian football' founding their league in 1891 and their football Association two years later. In his book *The Scottish World*, Billy Kay tells us that the very first Argentinian Championship in 1891 ended up with a play off between St Andrew's FC and Old Caledonians FC. To this day the official website of the Argentinian FA refers to '*Alejandro Watson Hutton, considerado con justicia "El Padre del Fútbol Argentino"*'.[68]

Many of these links were built through business, education and other endeavours. Even today you will find those with a connection to Scotland in South America. On a visit to Buenos Aires with the Foreign Affairs Committee a business dinner was held at the British Embassy. I sat next to a businessman who ran a chocolate company that produced Alfajores a popular Argentinian biscuit. He sat and spoke at length and with some pride of his Scottish ancestry, education and visits to the country including a love of golf. These were links that were to be found across the world and in many of the unlikeliest places.

* * *

One of these unlikely places where connections are to be found, and where this chapter started, is in the Caucasus, Europe's highest mountains. For centuries they have been at the crossroads of empires and to this day the imprint left by the Ottomans, Persians, Russians and Mongolians is apparent. There is even evidence of the brief British presence in the port of Batumi. The town on the Black Sea coast also hosts a statue of princess Medea who helped Jason and his argonauts steal the Golden Fleece from her father the local King.

As well as sitting at a crossroads for major powers the mountains can also be very remote. About 40 different indigenous languages are spoken in the Caucasus, more than any other part of the world save in Papua New Guinea and the Amazon. Whereas in the second two areas it is dense tropical forest that separates language groups in the Caucasus it is the mountains.[69] Unsurprisingly the Caucasus are known as the 'mountains of languages'.[70]

For any Scot who has visited the region the links are distinct and there will be some knowledge of our country at Europe's other extreme from the locals. The great Russian author, Mikhail Lermontov, referred to as the 'poet of the Caucasus', was part of the Scottish diaspora. His family were Learmonths from Fife and he was proud of his Scottish heritage. That pride is evident to visitors to his former home near Moscow today.

Lermontov was a Tsarist officer serving in the Caucasus during the Imperial campaigns there. He carried a Russian translation of Ossian's with him and made the connections between the place in which he was serving and his ancestral home. His poems have helped define how the Russians see the area.

In his book, *Black Sea*, Neal Ascherson recounts Lermontov's poem 'A Wish' where he becomes a raven and flies from the Caucasus to Scotland 'where the fields of my ancestors flower'. Ascherson describes it as Lermontov's 'vision of a Caucasian Scotland'. He also describes a meeting in the town of Anapa on the Black Sea coast bringing together a reunion or Learmonths and Lemontovs from Russia, Ukraine, France, the USA and even Dundee.[71]

Back in 2001 I was based in Georgia and there were still very few flights in and out of Tbilisi, the capital of Georgia, and few Westerners working in the city. Yet even here a small group of Scots were able to get together and arrange a Burns night to raise funds for local good causes. The links exist across the region and the former Soviet Union.

Being a Scot made travelling in the Caucasus slightly easier not least when crossing difficult 'borders'. I was able to discuss the merits of Burns in both Tbilisi with Georgians who had read his poetry in their own language and in Tskhinvali, capital of the breakaway entity of South Ossetia, where the 'Foreign Minister' had read Burns in Ossetian. I was also welcomed in both Baku, capital of Azerbaijan, and Yerevan, capital of Armenia, as well as Stepanakert, capital of the disputed Nagorno-Karabakh territory. In Baku there were especially strong links with Scotland and plenty of Scottish pubs in town to cater to thirsty oil and gas workers as well as locals. There was even an exchange rate for 'Scottish pounds' next to a Saltire advertised outside the local *bureaux de change*.

Historically the Scots have made a big impact on what was the Russian Empire. Brian Cox's TV series and Billy Kay's radio series are both excellent introductions to the impact of the Scots in Russia. Beyond the former Soviet Union in the rest of Europe one will find deep connections and an active Scottish diaspora.

Building and prospering from Scotland's links with its European diaspora is not a new idea. Scottish emigration across the Baltic was common in the 16th and 17th centuries. There was concern at home about the economic impact. A pamphlet published in 1695 warned that the migration of Scots to 'Ulster, the Scandinavian kingdoms, the Polish–Lithuanian Commonwealth, the Dutch Republic, England and her Atlantic colonies' had not meant Scotland prospering but the reverse.[72] The difficulty was that Scots were emigrating and occasionally finding great success in their new homes, but that wealth was not returning to Scotland. It didn't stop some organisations from trying to tap into the Scottish diaspora and between 1699 and 1703 Marischal College carried out two fundraising appeals:

> To all our generous and Charitable Countrey-men within the Cityes of Dantzick, and Konings-berg and the Kingdom of Poland for funds to renovate and rebuild.[73]

The appeal raised the substantial sum of £1,500 and shows that university fundraising efforts abroad are by no means a new phenomenon.

The diaspora communities across Europe may be older and even somewhat disconnected today but the links remain important. The European Single Market will continue to be the largest market for Scottish goods and services and its universities will continue to be important partners. Membership of the EU will trump any influence or connections that a diaspora community will have but it remains important as a source of connectivity and influence. The importance of relationships comes and goes, but a good diplomat will be able to build on those links that exist already to help with relationship building in the future.

The same goes for communities elsewhere in these islands. Just as the EU will remain Scotland's most important multi-lateral relationship so too will the relationship with the constituent parts of the UK and Ireland be crucial bilateral relationships.

It is here that the diaspora and family links will continue to be important as the relationship between the parts of these islands continues to evolve. The diaspora communities in Wales, England, Northern Ireland and the Republic of Ireland will be important in maintaining those ties in the future just as they are today.

* * *

Across the world states see their diasporas as an important part of their diplomatic toolbelt. That can be particularly important for smaller states as diasporas give them diplomatic clout through political and other influences. However, large states like China, Russia and India also use their diaspora for foreign policy ends. The latest UN data shows that those 'big' countries have the largest numbers of migrants.[74]

Different countries have varying policies towards their diasporas. This will depend on their foreign policy goals and ambitions as well as the nature of the diaspora community. The clearest example of another diaspora where Scotland might draw lessons is of course Ireland. Diaspora policy has been a major part of Irish foreign policy since well before Irish independence. The global Irish community played an important role in Ireland's emerging role in international affairs.

Like Scotland, this was particularly evident in the USA. Addressing the Dáil Éireann in June 1963 John F Kennedy spoke of the leaflets that Benjamin Franklin had sent to 'Irish Freedom Fighters' and the influence that Irish leader Robert Emmet had on US President Abraham Lincoln and George Washington had on Daniel O'Connell. He told Irish parliamentarians that day: 'No people ever believed more deeply in the cause of Irish freedom than the people of the United States.'[75]

He was speaking just 40 years after Ireland's independence and 25 years after the founding of the Irish Republic and, as he told the Irish parliamentarians, 83 years after Parnell had addressed the US Congress. Even back in 1919 a resolution had been passed in Congress calling on the US delegation to Versailles to make the case for Irish self-determination.[76]

President Kennedy highlighted Ireland's internationalism looking ahead to its potential membership of the European Community and praised its influence at the UN as 'far greater than your relative size'. The US President, the leader of the free world, told Ireland:

> This has never been a rich or powerful country, and yet, since earliest times, its influence on the world has been rich and powerful.

Even today the Irish Taoiseach is one of the few national leaders absolutely guaranteed an annual meeting with the US President on St Patrick's Day every year when the US head of state will be seen sporting a green tie. It is good for Ireland and good politics for the occupant of the White House.

On 4 July 2020 the Irish Embassy in Washington DC tweeted 'Happy 4 July to the 10.1% of American residents of Irish ancestry. And to the 89.9% who aren't. No friendship matters more to us.' That is a powerful message and delivers significant clout.

The premium that Ireland places on its 70 million strong diaspora today is clear from its Foreign Ministry which invests strongly in the relationship. We see the importance that is attached to this part of Ireland's Foreign policy muscle:

> Ireland is lucky to have a diaspora who makes a meaningful contribution to our country, whether they're building economic development, raising awareness of our culture or creating a positive image of Ireland in their adopted homes.

We're committed to recognising their efforts by engaging
with them both practically and strategically.[77]

The focus and thinking around engaging with the diaspora is clear
from a glance at the website under a section entitled the 'Irish Abroad'.
There are links to 'Your Irish Heritage' helping members find any lost
great-grannies and assistance for the 'most vulnerable of our emigrants' with an Emigrant Support Programme, maintaining links and
help for those who have left Ireland. There details about the Global
Irish Network that meets in and helps Ireland's network of embassies
and consulates and information about the 'Presidential Award' for
services to Ireland by those living abroad. Importantly there is information on 'Returning to Ireland to Live' with helpful tips for those
returning home.

So here we have some simple and straight forward assistance for
those abroad, maintaining and strengthening the ties to the diaspora.
It means that Ireland does not leave you when you step off the island.
For a country that, like Scotland, has seen generations of its brightest
and best leave home investing in help for those who want to return
makes sense. Those returnees will have skills, experience and networks that they would never have developed had they not left. The
diaspora is valuable to Ireland wherever it is to be found overseas
but it is perhaps even more valuable when its members return.

A returning diaspora brings significant economic benefits. Scotland's
links with the diaspora have been flagged as an area where an independent Scotland could encourage more immigration given its own demo-
graphic challenges. In written evidence to the Foreign Affairs Committee
Inquiry into Scottish independence ahead of the 2014 Independence
Referendum Professor Whitman and Dr Andrew Blick of the University
of Kent told MPs that on immigration:

a more liberal policy by Scotland, perhaps involving the
encouragement of inward migration from within the Scottish
diaspora, would create difficulties for the rump UK.[78]

And that one of the downsides of independence for the UK as a whole
could be less contact with the Scottish diaspora. That said there appears
to be precious little engagement with the Scottish diaspora by the
Foreign Office.

Across the Irish sea our neighbours look set to build on their links. At time of writing the Irish are developing a new diaspora policy:

> Ireland is fortunate in having a diaspora of 70 million people around the world. Our relationship with this global community is something we should cherish and celebrate. Global Ireland: Ireland's Global Footprint to 2025 – the Government's plan to double our international presence – commits us to introducing a new diaspora policy in 2020. This new policy will guide Ireland's engagement and relationship with our diaspora: our emigrants, our citizens abroad, those of Irish heritage and those who feel an affinity with Ireland around the world.[79]

Working with the diaspora is clearly a priority and Ireland does not simply focus on the rich and powerful. This year the Irish Foreign Ministry says it will spend over €12.5 million on its Emigrant Support Programme. Upon taking office after the Irish Government Coalition Agreement on 2 July 2020 the new Minister for the Diaspora, Dublin TD Colm Brophy, highlighted the importance of the diaspora in his first statement as Minister saying:

> Strong diaspora communities play a key role in helping to promote a positive awareness of Ireland, Irish culture and heritage around the world. My focus in the coming months and years will be to listen to, and to support, our diaspora communities, particularly its most vulnerable members.[80]

In July 2020 *The Economist* ran an article entitled 'How Ireland gets its way – an unlikely diplomatic superpower'.[81] That article highlights Ireland's diplomatic successes in recent years. It highlights the range of good work that Ireland delivers as part of its foreign policy with the Irish in key positions of influence around the world including within the EU institutions:

> Ireland has some natural advantages. A history of emigration blessed it with a huge diaspora in America, which unlike say the German diaspora, is vocal about its heritage. That ensures an audience in the White House and sway on Capitol Hill. It is a small, English-speaking country with diplomats able to focus on a few clear aims. A policy of neutrality helps

it avoid unpopular military entanglement. Unlike most rich European countries, it carries no imperial baggage. Indeed, Ireland's history as a victim of colonialism still provides a useful icebreaker with countries once coloured pink on Victorian maps. Nor is Ireland shy about using its cultural clout.

There has been criticism in the past that Ireland's efforts are simply 'shamrock diplomacy'. Those critics would do well to learn from Ireland's success. Perhaps for the first time in history, Dublin finds itself in a more influential position than London diplomatically. Certainly, on Brexit, *The Economist* article highlighted that 'the EU's position on Brexit was shaped by Irish diplomats'. In Washington Nancy Pelosi warned that any US/UK trade deal would have 'no chance' if it undermined the Good Friday Agreement.[82] She was later backed up by then US presidential candidate Joe Biden. The new Presidential administration have been clear in their support for Dublin and the Good Friday Agreement. Amanda Sloat who joined Biden's White House administration told me that 'there has been a lot of support in DC for preserving the peace process in Northern Ireland' during the Brexit process.

Unsurprisingly the UK Government and pro-Brexit MPs have felt threatened by this progress. I remember speaking to a normally thoughtful Tory MP in the parliamentary lobby about the ongoing Brexit mess in 2017. Recent negotiations had seen the UK isolated and the EU27 united behind Ireland. 'The boggies better not mess this up for us', he whispered giving away some of the attitudes that persist. It is a lack of understanding of the Good Friday Agreement, our relationship with the EU and Dublin's international clout that have consistently led to avoidable problems for Brexiteers.

Ireland has worked hard on its diplomacy over the years and the results have been seen with diplomatic successes in Brussels, Washington DC, New York and Berlin. Years of working away at relationships, a commitment to international organisations have paid off for this 'diplomatic superpower'. The Irish recognised early that Brexit posed one of the gravest threats to the Republic's national interest as well as the peace process in Northern Ireland which is so important to that country and its citizens who live on both sides of the border. Based on hard work over years Ireland's diplomats and politicians were able to step up to the unprecedented challenge.

***

Ireland is the most informative place for Scotland when it comes to learning lessons in terms of diaspora engagement. It rightly gets the most attention from decision makers and commentators. Other countries do pursue their own diaspora policies and it is worth some reflection.

The investment that the diaspora community had made in Armenia's physical infrastructure, including roads mentioned at the start of this chapter, was just one contribution. Armenians were spread throughout the world at the end of the First World War having suffered dreadful atrocities in the areas that they lived that went well beyond the borders of the modern state. Those atrocities have been described as a genocide and resulted in Armenians leaving their homes behind. As a consequence, there is now a vibrant and widespread global community who have built links and sought to assist the country since it gained independence from the Soviet Union in 1991.

The relationship that the Armenian diaspora has with the state is difficult and somewhat complex. Historically the role of the community was focused on preserving the identity of the Armenian people as well as on 'genocide recognition'. After independence the need to support the new state in the chaos of the collapse of the former Soviet Union also provided an important role for the diaspora.

That was given added urgency by a devastating earthquake in 1988 in the country and the outbreak of a bloody war with neighbouring Azerbaijan over Nagorno-Karabakh. Today the National Security Strategy of Armenia has highlighted the important role of diaspora relations with a Foreign Policy Centre report stating:

> the National Security Strategy of the Republic of Armenia officially identified 'Armenia-Diaspora relations' as a 'significant component' of national security and recognised the role of the diaspora as offering 'a serious degree of economic and cultural potential, especially as a means to promote trade, tourism, preservation, development and publicizing of the

cultural heritage...to foster Armenia's global integration and consolidation of democracy'.[83]

The powerful role of the Armenian diaspora has been displayed across the world. France was the first country to recognise the massacre of Armenians at the end of the war as genocide. In 2019 President Macron marked the first 'national day of commemoration on the Armenian genocide' fulfilling a campaign commitment to the Armenian diaspora in 2017.[84]

The recognition of the genocide might seem unremarkable were it not for Ankara's intense diplomatic efforts around the issue that sees such recognition as an attack on Turkey. In July 2020 a diplomatic spat was provoked when a White House spokeswoman referred to the genocide and found her comments praised by Armenian groups and criticised by Turkey.[85]

This is regularly played out in Washington DC where the Armenian diaspora is seen by some as being second only to the Israeli in terms of its power and influence. It is much better organised than those from Azerbaijan or Turkey with grassroots networks in key swing states. Back in 1992 the diaspora even had Azerbaijan struck off a list of countries eligible for US aid. In August 2006 it used its influence to stop the confirmation of Ambassador-designate Richard Hoagland because of his failure to recognise the genocide as such.[86] In 2019 Armenia also saw a 40 per cent uplift in funds from the US Foreign Assistance Budget after lobbying from the diaspora.

In the recent conflict in Nagorno-Karabakh the Armenian diaspora was much more influential than those of Azerbaijan or Turkey especially with the Biden campaign. Vice-President Kamala Harris comes from California with a strong diaspora community. Famous American-Armenians such as Kim Kardashian and Cher, born Cherilyn Sarkisian, got behind support for Armenia. However, there have been criticisms of the diaspora who can sometimes take a harder line which is easier to do in the comfort of Los Angeles than it is in the area affected by conflict.[87]

* * *

Diasporas globally carry political influence that can be used for political, economic and diplomatic purposes. Cubans play a powerful role in the USA's politics not least in the swing state of Florida where the Cuban and Venezuelan communities were said to have been an important factor in helping deliver the state for Trump in the 2020 Presidential elections.[88] Many members of the Iraqi diaspora reportedly played a key role in encouraging the Iraq conflict and removal of Saddam ahead of the war in 2003.[89]

This happens for a range of foreign policy actors and as a Member of Parliament I can remember being emailed by Cypriot constituents (with template emails) to highlight their concerns around what they saw as illegal Turkish drilling in Cypriot territorial waters. In terms of economics countries such as India, the Philippines, Mexico and others with migrant communities recognise the contributions they make domestically through financial remittances back home.[90]

In business diasporas can give you an 'in' to the market providing contacts and expertise. Culture can play a critical role in building business and other partnerships where diasporas can act as a bridge between communities having an insight with both. In a book for the World Bank Yuri Kuznetzov wrote:

> knowledge and expertise of both global opportunities and local particulars; and, frequently, financial resources to act on new opportunities, the contributions of diasporas can be spectacular.[91]

He went on to illustrate his point with an example of where the Korean diaspora in the USA were able to be more helpful to Samsung than the South Korean Government. The diaspora deployed a light touch approach to engagement that helped the company gain licences for key technologies where an intensive government led intervention had failed.

Newly independent states have also looked to their diasporas with state-building in recent times. The Baltic states have been incredibly successful in recent years emerging from the stagnation of Soviet rule. They went from Moscow's control to full membership of the European Union in just a few years. Part of that achievement was due to successful diaspora engagement.

Estonia's Compatriots Programme managed by the Ministries of Education and Culture reaches out with language teaching and other events abroad. There is also assistance for returning Estonians who can qualify for a payment from the Integration and Migration Foundation. Information is provided in English, Russian and Estonian and you can book a consultation to talk about your 'return home'.[92]

In Lithuania the Ministry of Foreign Affairs has worked on its 'Global Lithuania diaspora programme' and appointed an Ambassador at Large for the Lithuanian community in 2012. The Foreign Minister at the time even travelled to a gathering of Lithuanian American community in Atlanta where he said: 'Lithuania and its diaspora are one united undivided and indivisible family.'[93]

Latvia has engaged with its diaspora and allowed dual-citizenship for those living in EU and NATO Member States as well as Latvians with Australian, Brazilian and New Zealand passports.[94]

In Croatia the first post-independence President of the country Franjo Tudjman received $4 million in donations for his campaign from countrymen abroad. The diaspora was considered to have been rewarded afterwards with 12 of the 120 seats in the Croat Parliament going to Croatians overseas, more than for Croatia's minority groups.[95] This has now been reduced with just three MPs representing the diaspora constituency compared to eight for minority groups.[96]

In developing states diaspora communities can have a powerful role to play. That is often driven by emotion especially countries that are newly independent or emerging from authoritarian regimes where the community may have been victims of repression. This can provide an important source of international clout and much needed expertise.

Closer to home, states cultivate their diaspora communities even in the most developed countries. In the European Union for example some Permanent Representations (Member State embassies to the EU) will engage with those working in the institutions. This even includes sub-state actors and Scots working in the institutions regularly attend events at Scotland House. There are also more informal networks such as that around the Danish Church in Brussels or the monthly musical *seisún* at the James Joyce pub near the EU Commission headquarters that attracts members of the Irish community and their friends from across the European institutions.

Governments do not always have such a positive and benign relationship with their diaspora communities. Some authorities have taken action to bring difficult diaspora community members to heel. The attempted murder of Sergei Skripal and his daughter by Russian agents in Salisbury was an attempt by the Kremlin to send a powerful message out to Russians that it didn't matter where you lived. Even if you were no longer a Russian citizen you were not beyond the reach of the Kremlin. Those actions also led to the death of UK citizen Dawn Sturgess who had nothing to do with Russia. Chechen dissidents have also been targeted with murders of diaspora members in Germany, Austria and France for example.

Similarly, Jamal Khashoggi was brutally murdered inside the Saudi Arabian Consulate in Istanbul. He was a journalist who, like Skripal, had been close to the regime but was later critical. His murder was also a chilling message to the diaspora community members who criticised the Saudi Government. So with political influence also comes a threat and it can be difficult for former nationals to truly leave behind authoritarian regimes even when they move abroad and gain citizenship of liberal democracies.[97] On a visit to Turkey with the Foreign Affairs Committee, the President, Prime Minister and other officials repeatedly raised the need for the extradition of Fetullah Gülen who has lived in the United States since 1999. Turkish authorities accused him of being behind the attempted coup that had taken place a short time before our visit.

* * *

Scotland's relationship with its diaspora, like those of other countries, is not quite so testy or likely to ever be so. It is a community that is, so far, keen to get involved and help without feeling the need for a political say. The author Neal Ascherson described Scotland's diaspora as 'politically quite useless'. He is right and that is not such a bad thing. Surely Scotland's politics should be left to those who live and work here regardless of where they are from.

Those who will be most affected by the political decisions that are made about Scotland are those who live here. That was the mandate in the 2014 Independence Referendum and should be the mandate now. Attempts to set the mandate by means of ethnicity or birth would be not only fraught with difficulty (identifying who counts) but also a deeply uncomfortable experience of anyone who believes in the civic nature of the state and Scottish identity.

The focus of this work is rightly on business links. Ascherson picked up on this theme in his book on the Black Sea where he commends the SNP's efforts to avoid ethnic nationalism much to the chagrin of the late Conservative MP for Perth and Kinross Nicholas Fairbairn who complained that any '"Greek, Tasmanian or the bastard child of an American serviceman" would have more rights in Scotland than an emigrant of pure Scots descent.'[98] In our inter-connected world surely that is the way forward? If our diaspora is a civic one, then the state should be as well.

Scotland's network of offices would act as a useful focal point for the diaspora. Scotland House in Brussels regularly attracts Scots working in the institutions as well as those with an affinity for Scotland. That has already helped build up a useful network, one that will be more important than ever before in the post-Brexit era. Other offices can serve a similar function though of course in a limited way since they do not have diplomatic resources or status.

Since the re-establishment of the Scottish Parliament efforts on diaspora engagement have largely focused on economic development, with some success. Scottish institutions have undertaken some good work on re-engaging with the diaspora. Holyrood administrations deserve credit by recognising and making the most of this opportunity.

GlobalScot was set up by the Scottish Executive in 2001 and is focused on growing the economy and Scotland's global connections. It was described as 'an international business network of Scots and people with an affinity for Scotland'. The programme won praise from a World Bank Institute book on diaspora networks in 2006 cited as an example of best practice.[99] Today the network is still in operation with a high acceptance rate for participation though there are questions around whether it is still the right vehicle to ensure that membership is 'optimal'.[100] Even back in 2006 there were questions as to the extent that GlobalScot could expand given the limited support that could be provided backed up in 2006 administered by a team of five in Scottish Enterprise.[101]

A report published by Momentous Change Ltd. took the views of the business diaspora. The study was able to measure the views of 1067 business diaspora Scots from 74 countries around the world.

That alone illustrated the appetite for engagement among the business community.

It was revealing that Scotland is viewed positively among the diaspora and key descriptors of the country being 'friendly, progressive, resilient, entrepreneurial, progressive and outward looking'. The respondents also demonstrated a willingness to further help Scotland's business community and 'contribute their knowledge and experience to support the growth of international trade'.[102]

Those findings show that there is further opportunity to be had. It was striking that the report defined the diaspora widely as 'those who are born Scottish, have worked, studied or have some family connections with Scotland'. Interestingly it also allowed participants to describe themselves as 'affinity Scots' who may have studied, worked or have some other 'non-ethnic relationship to Scotland'. They made up about a quarter of respondents and the authors posed the question as to whether we should consider the diaspora as being civic in nature rather than ethnic. That was an incredibly positive finding and one that is being embraced.

Given the size of Scotland's diaspora working with it will always be a major undertaking since governments have limited resources. Scotland's population relative to its diaspora means that there will always be a challenge however it may be time to re-consider that engagement as part of our future foreign policy.

I spoke to Roger Mullin about his report and he told me that the diaspora represents a massive asset but 'we could do a lot more' to tap into that resource and that it cannot simply be left up to the agencies who he said could at times be somewhat 'risk averse'. That should include engaging with recent emigrants as well as the more established diaspora who are 'through their own initiative engaging with Scotland'.

A report comparing Ireland and Scotland found that even though Scotland has had some success in building links with the diaspora it is 'almost as expansive and large as the Irish diaspora and is a huge and relatively untapped resource for Scotland'. Ireland has the same challenges in terms of the size and widespread nature of the diaspora and is praised for having a 'light and flexible structure' and so gives much ownership to its members.[103]

Scotland does have a significant disadvantage in not having a Foreign Ministry of its own. In other countries there is a ready-made focal point for the diaspora through their diplomatic representations. Within the UK, Scotland's taxpayers contribute to the UK Embassy network where there is little evidence of any meaningful interaction with the diaspora. In a recent response to a parliamentary question about engagement with the diaspora the Foreign Office responded that there had been some Burns suppers held, the odd Saltire flown and some activity on social media to promote Scotland. The focus of the Foreign Office was on the 'Britain is Great' campaign parliament was told.[104]

Interestingly the response highlighted the three European embassies that had held Burns suppers being those in Riga, Tbilisi and Budapest. These dinners are a valuable soft power tool for the UK to reach out to local stakeholders and incidentally all three embassies mentioned were headed by a Scottish Ambassador at the time.

There are others who think that the UK could make more of the diaspora. Former Conservative MEP and prominent Brexit supporter David Campbell Bannerman suggested to me that the UK could 'use the Scottish diaspora to get into the pro-British service markets at a (US) state level'. He was suggesting that the UK cultivates the Scottish diaspora in the US states to help the UK deliver its message beyond Washington DC.

The UK Government appears to be apprehensive about engaging with the diaspora as the answer to the parliamentary question illustrated. David Clark a former Special Adviser to Robin Cook when he was Foreign Secretary, spoke about the Scottish diaspora being there but not finding the same 'level of expression' as the Irish. He told me that 'is because Ireland is an independent state with a Foreign Ministry of its own' and that 'an independent Scotland would obviously be able to provide the same kind of focus as Ireland, including the allocation of specific resources'.

Others, such as Washington DC based Scot Amy MacKinnon, talked about the catching up that Scotland must do on our Irish neighbours.

In the SNP there is a recognition now that there has been more that could have been done on the diaspora. In her autobiography, *Stop the World*, Winnie Ewing wrote:

> I have always felt that the SNP could gain great strength from
> the diaspora, particularly Canada and America, and I do feel

that as a party we have failed to capitalise on the support we have from such places.[105]

Long serving SNP Cabinet Secretary Michael Russell acknowledges that more could be done by the Scottish Government. I think it is fair to say that the government is doing what it can with limited resources and without an embassy network. There is a two-way conversation to be had on how Scotland interacts with and uses its diaspora. Michael Russell says that there could be a problem with the 'shortbread tin approach'. There has been progress such as the Congressional Friends of Scotland and the European Parliament Friends of Scotland but as he says, 'we have work to do on the diaspora'.

The Scottish Government White Paper that was produced ahead of the Independence Referendum did have some good ideas. When discussing how a diplomatic presence might look the paper set out that an independent Scotland would:

> appoint members of the Scottish diaspora and prominent local people as honorary consuls to represent Scottish interests in nations where there is no direct Scottish representation.

That strikes me as a good and innovative idea and one that is already practiced in Edinburgh by states with limited resources and no direct representation in the capital and other major cities.

* * *

Diaspora engagement goes both ways and Scotland benefits from the presence of several diaspora communities made up of those who have made their home here. Since earliest times Scotland has seen waves of both emigration and immigration. Our nation has been enhanced and enriched by those who have made the country their home. Historian Tom Devine wrote in 2015 that 'Scots should be proud to belong to a mongrel nation'.[106]

Professor Devine is right we should be proud of our diversity. Not only does diversity enrich our economy, political life and society at home it also provides reach internationally. In his speech at the Brookings Institute in 2013 Alex Salmond spoke of the impact of the diasporas:

we have different approaches in international rela-
ɔr different countries. Our friendship with Pakistan is
on the large diaspora which makes a significant con-
ɔn to modern Scotland. Our ties to China and India
have developed through shared economic interests, as well
as the links between our peoples.'

More recently the Refugees Welcome campaign has been important
in helping those fleeing conflict feel at home here. Sabir Zazai, the
Chief Executive of the Scottish Refugee Council, who was himself
a refugee from Afghanistan, told me that 'this is a place you can
rebuild your life in safety and dignity and be proud of your new
home'. For refugees who have suffered so much 'it's about feeling
at home'. When we think of the massive contributions that refugees
have made to their new homes over the centuries, we see the importance of welcoming new Scots who have left their countries of origin
in the most appalling circumstances.

Those links that the diaspora communities in Scotland have will
continue to be crucial especially since the UK decision to leave the EU.
Scots who happen to hold the passport of an EU state are as much part
of the nation as any other group. A clear message about the status
of concerned EU nationals never emerged from Downing Street but
did come from the steps of Bute House just hours after the result of
the EU Referendum. At that unsettling time Nicola Sturgeon sought
immediate guarantees for EU nationals from the British Government
and told those citizens 'you are welcome here, Scotland is your home
and your contribution is valued'.

There were those who criticised her saying that nothing would
change but it has since become evident just how much these words
were needed and welcomed. I received countless messages from EU
nationals both constituents and friends who were grateful for those
words. It is easy to forget that politics and what is said affects people's lives and the EU Referendum had a deeply unsettling impact
on EU citizens living in the UK.

Italians, Poles, Lithuanians along with people from the rest of
the British islands and the rest of Europe have made and continue
to make a huge contribution to Scotland. Many also retain links to
their countries of origin. As part of his election campaign back in
2007 the leader of the opposition and future Polish and EU leader

Donald Tusk campaigned in Kirkcaldy where he held a rally and told the BBC that the Scottish diaspora was 'crucial'.[107]

As we sit at a crossroads in Scotland's future, we know that we cannot lose those links. It is right that the Scottish diaspora should not have a say in how we decide on our future but and that any 'Greek, Tasmanian or the bastard child of an American serviceman' who has made Scotland their home should.

There is significant potential with Scotland's diaspora overseas as well as those communities here. Both are a massive asset to our nation and unlocking its international potential. That will be important as the country seeks to further build its links across Europe and the rest of the world. If Scotland remains in the UK that is also important for the whole of the UK. However, it would be an even bigger resource for a newly independent state, if fully harnessed, as others in a similar position have found.

CHAPTER 3

Foreign Policy Without a Foreign Ministry

International relations, including relations with territories outside the United Kingdom, the European Union (and their institutions) and other international organisations, regulation of international trade, and international development assistance and co-operation are reserved matters.

Scotland Act 1998, Schedule 5, Section 7(1) setting out powers reserved to Westminster

THE SCOTLAND ACT establishing the Scottish Parliament was quite explicit: foreign affairs were reserved to Westminster and were not the business of the devolved administration. Even so, since its establishment the Parliament has debated international affairs and successive administrations have had external relations policies. This was also the case with secretaries of state for Scotland who would engage with Scotland's international profile including in EU affairs before the restoration of the Scottish Parliament in 1999.

In 2003 the Scottish Parliament debated the Iraq War with the political correspondent John Knox describing it as 'the best parliamentary debate of the year so far'.[108] The Labour Party were joined by the Conservatives in helping secure backing for the Westminster Government's actions but Labour's coalition partners, the Liberal Democrats, backed the SNP motion in opposition to the invasion.

Throughout the devolution period all First Ministers have been keen to promote the country on the world stage. There was a divergence when different parties held power in Holyrood and Westminster but even before then there was a distinctive attempt to engage in international relations when the same party held office in both.

Right from the outset this was the case. When you come out of the elevator at Scotland House in Brussels there is still a plaque to Donald Dewar who opened those offices. They sit in the very heart of the Europe quarter in Brussels and, as anyone who works there will tell you, the Saltire is the only flag to fly on Rond Pont Schuman directly opposite the European Commission's Berlaymont headquarters.

There was also a willingness to engage with the devolved institutions among Scotland's friends and neighbours. In the very first words spoken at the reconvening of the Scottish Parliament on 12 May 1999 Winnie Ewing talked of Scotland's place in the world and referred to the 'bank of goodwill' that existed towards Scotland in the international community. The new Scottish Parliament received gifts from other parliaments including Iceland, Norway and the Netherlands. Iceland's contribution, by artist Sigurður Guðmundsson, is a pink footed goose egg (in granite), a bird that spends its winters in Scotland and summers in Iceland, engraved with the words 'With laws the land shall be built'. It is set on lava rock taken from the site of Iceland's former Parliament at *Thingvellir* that started meeting 1100 years ago.

> Jack McConnell spoke of an ambition to be 'outward looking' right from the very start and spoke of his ambition for the 'Scottish Parliament and Scottish Government' to be engaged with the outside world. The former First Minister even reached back in history telling the Institute for Government: 'I felt the best of Scotland over the centuries had been outward looking and engaged internationally, and I thought we should do that.'[109]

Since coming to power the SNP has sought to pursue its own foreign policy agenda and one that is distinct from the UK. This is naturally restricted by what the Scottish Government can do under the Scotland Act. However, its External Affairs Directorate sets out its responsibilities as:

- enhancing Scotland's international relationships
- promoting Scotland's ambition to be a good global citizen

- protecting our place and interests in Europe
- influencing migration policies for Scotland's distinct needs.[110]

Scotland's foreign policy footprint is to be found hiding in plain sight. The Scottish Parliament regularly engages internationally and debates foreign affairs subjects, some of which could be argued to be within the Parliament's remit, others patently not. This international affairs footprint has been brought into sharp focus by the UK's decision to leave the EU, a move that has met with strong resistance in Scotland.

A quick glance at the Scottish Government's 'International' webpages illustrates the scope of the work being undertaken. There is information on areas as diverse as the Scottish Government's approach to Europe, international development and international relations. The government has produced strategies on engagement with China, India, the USA and the Arctic among others. There is also information about some of the Scottish Government's overseas offices including those in Washington DC, Brussels, Paris, Berlin, Dublin and Beijing.[111]

There is clearly a desire to develop this work. The appointment in 2019 of Scott Wightman shows deepening engagement and a bolstering of the Scottish Government's diplomatic skills set. Mr Wightman was appointed Director of External Affairs in 2019 after a high-flying career of 36 years in the British diplomatic service including spells as Ambassador in Seoul and the High Commissioner to Singapore.

That diplomatic know-how is incredibly important and quite distinct from those who have worked in other areas such as economic development. Another important appointment has been the Head of the Dublin office, John Webster, who moved to the Scottish Government from the British Embassy in Ireland. When I visited the Dáil and met with politicians from across the political spectrum, it was clear just how well connected and highly regarded he is. One senior Irish politician told me in reference to John: 'Having a trained diplomat in this country makes a huge difference'. Mr Webster's work makes him a major asset in engaging with Scotland's closest EU neighbour and important partner.

Scotland is no different from other sub-state actors in having a foreign policy footprint that seeks to have its voice heard in the international arena. The relationship with the state entity is incredibly important and varies from country to country. The UK is very centralised compared to other similar states and culturally the Foreign Office appears to have a challenge even contemplating that Scotland has a distinctive international footprint.

Many sub-state entities have a much more developed and formalised external affairs role. Scotland has made progress since 1999 and there are areas where Scotland has acted and had a distinctive approach in international affairs. There is strong brand recognition and political clout with states starting to think about Scotland's role and taking the prospect of independence seriously. But there is still much to be done and much of the thinking on foreign affairs is still underdeveloped as Cabinet Secretary Michael Russell acknowledged.

* * *

International development and a role helping the world's poorest and most vulnerable has been important to all First Ministers. McConnell believed that his work to promote investment in Scotland should be matched with an effort to 'give something back'. He continues to campaign on the Sustainable Development Goals, and we travelled to the UN together in 2019 as part of that campaign along with colleagues from other parties and humanitarian NGOs. He explained his thinking to me:

> Every level of government should reduce conflict and inequality around the world. But there is no point in simply replicating the work of the Foreign Office, each level of government can find its own purpose.

The Scotland Act clearly reserved international development to UK Government. However, McConnell and the Scottish Executive Chief Economist Andrew Goudie, who had held the same post at the Department for International Development, used the Scotland Act provision that it could act 'to advance the interest of the UK Government'. He was supported by the then UK International Development Secretary, Labour's Hilary Benn, who had said that 'when it comes to ending global poverty, there is more than enough work to go-round'.

Ever since then Scottish Government's work in international development has grown. It maintains a 'special relationship' with Malawi but has also supported programmes in Pakistan, Rwanda, Zambia and elsewhere. There has been some fantastic work due to the Scotland Malawi partnership and agreement that it is helpful to some of the world's poorest. With such a comparatively small budget it makes sense to focus the work in a country with a strong connection to Scotland.

There is much to be learned from the work in Malawi. David Hope-Jones of the Scotland Malawi partnership describes the relationship as having a 'sense of partnership beyond the norms of development'. The depth of the relationship and links that have been developed over the years is unquestionable. They have been well outlined in the book *Malawi and Scotland: Together in the Talking Place Since 1859* by Kenneth Ross (Mzuni Press, 2013) that reflects on this special and deep relationship. A recent event to discuss the partnership brought together 250 different organisations and a senior EU diplomat in Malawi telling David: 'Scotland's got something none of us have in this place.' It is difficult to imagine a similar relationship between two modestly sized countries thousands of miles apart.

However there is some gentle criticism from those working in the NGO sector. It is seen by some within international development sector as being 'parochial' and another said the work on 'Malawi is fine but a bit narrowly focused, we could do so much more'. There is consensus that the work should continue but perhaps as part of broader efforts and for Scotland to find its own expertise and specialisms in International Aid just as other similar sized countries have done.

There is some agreement that Scotland should have a role in international development across the political divide in Scotland. The debate in Holyrood is quite distinctive from that at Westminster where there has been criticism of aid spend of any sort in the media and on the Conservative benches. That would be unthinkable across the Scottish Parliament. It is certainly difficult to see serious politicians in Scotland suggesting that the aid budget be cut and some of the money spent on a new Royal Yacht as was the case at Westminster.[112]

Those differences were underlined in a debate on the Royal Yacht where some MPs even thought it would be the answer to the UK's Brexit difficulties. The Conservative MP Jake Berry secured a debate in Parliament on 11 October 2016 entitled *Royal Yacht Britannia: International Trade* where he argued for a yacht to boost trade and argued that Parliament had to consider what to do 'to make Britain great again'. It was suggested that some of the funding for the suggested yacht should come from the Department of International Development.

During that debate the Member for Edinburgh North and Leith, the MP for the Royal Yacht Britannia, caused some controversy by referring to the yacht as 'it' during her remarks. There was an unhappy reaction to the SNP MP's remarks from Conservative MPS. The following exchange sums up the frustration that many of us had over the level of debate in the House of Commons on these issues at times.

> Deidre Brock (Edinburgh North and Leith) (SNP): I declare
> an interest of sorts: Britannia is moored in my constituency.
> It is not going anywhere, partly because one of its propellers
> has been melted down and is now in the form of a statue of
> a yottie, or royal yachtsman, and partly because it is owned
> privately by a trust; it is not in public hands.

> Mr James Gray (North Wiltshire) (Con): The hon. Lady
> might show true respect to the Royal Yacht Britannia if she
> described it not as 'it' but as 'she'.[113]

* * *

Another area where there has been a foreign policy divergence between London and Edinburgh has been around climate change. By a quirk of legislative drafting the issue is the responsibility of the Scottish Parliament. Schedule 5 of the Scotland Act sets out the powers that are reserved, but not devolved. When that Act was being drafted back in 1997 climate change was not included for the simple reason that very few people were discussing and debating the issue and, at the time, it was not deemed worthy of being reserved.

When it came to tackling climate change the Scottish Parliament found itself in a position to make ground-breaking legislation. The Parliament at the time was also one of minorities with the SNP, the governing party, holding 47 seats out of 129 just one more seat than the Labour Party. As the Special Adviser on Climate Change in 2009 I found myself shuttling between parties, businesses, environmental groups and academics among others as consensus was sought.

To be fair Ministers, especially John Swinney and Stewart Stevenson, and other MSPs, were seeking to be ambitious but it was civic Scotland that played a critical role in the passing of the Climate Change Act 2009. The key groups were speaking to each other and using their leverage with all the political parties on the legislation. That brought together environmental groups' campaigning prowess, academics' excellence, businesses' finance and commercial expertise together to make the case for ambitious targets. The fact that the government was in a minority and relied on other parties for support also helped.

In the end the Scottish Government's Act with a world-leading 42 per cent reduction in greenhouse gas emissions by 2020 on a 1990 baseline was passed. The STUC (Scottish Trade Union Congress) and CBI (Confederation of British Industry) both got behind it and even the Conservatives backed the Act. I remember the late, and decent, MSP Alex Johnstone, then his party's environment spokesperson, telling me of his party's decision on the morning of the final vote. The Bill was passed unanimously.

This was delivered despite strong civil service advice against the target of 42 per cent being set. Some argued that the Parliament should stick with the less ambitious targets being pursued at Westminster under its 2008 Climate Change Act. That had important consequences. Not only had Scotland passed world-leading climate change legislation but had done so unanimously with backing from Scottish business, academics and others who would have to do much of that hard work to deliver the targets. It was also a powerful narrative of cross sector action and multi-party agreement to tell the rest of the world.

A significant opportunity to tell that story came later in 2009 with the UN Climate Change Conference, COP15, in Copenhagen. With the passing of the Act Scotland was rapidly gaining recognition as a leader on climate change. That had very little traction in Whitehall and a request by the Scottish Government for the First Minister to join the UK delegation was refused, although one Scottish Government civil servant was permitted to join. Alex Salmond went there anyway to promote Scotland and its climate ambitions saying:

just because we are not in the best position at present should not prevent us establishing a good position in enhancing Scotland's international profile.

Salmond's attendance was welcomed by environmental campaigners who joined him in Copenhagen including Richard Dixon, director of WWF Scotland, who had been instrumental in building the case for the Scottish Act:

Scotland's climate legislation is a great example at a time when the world desperately needs good examples. Even though Scotland has been denied the opportunity to be part of the official UK delegation, it really is great news that the First Minister will now be going to Copenhagen.[114]

It was not universally welcomed with the Conservative spokesperson criticising his attendance saying:

The First Minister tried to use his trip to Copenhagen at the taxpayers' expense to boost his own ego and the SNP's falling poll ratings rather than as a serious attempt to tackle climate change.[115]

Salmond made a success of the visit and put Scotland on the map in Copenhagen even though he was not part of the official UK delegation. This included the signing of an agreement with President Nasheed of the Maldives that was 'focused on [the] close friendly relationship that exists between Scotland and the Maldives' such as work on renewables and education according to the Maldives' Government notice.[116] There was concrete action with the important message that this was an agreement between the industrialised nation that had the most ambitious targets and the nation that most needed help being the low lying islands of that Indian Ocean country.

There was also an initiative by the environmental groups to give 42 per cent proof bottles of whisky to world leaders. Seeing an opportunity Alex Salmond threatened to water down the whisky if leaders watered down their commitment. The trip to Copenhagen was a success but instead of harnessing Scotland's story the UK had distanced themselves from a good news message from a part of the UK. It was a political decision not to include Scotland's First Minister. The UK Government could have benefitted from Scotland's inclusion in its team but chose not to, it also meant that Alex Salmond could set his own timetable and agenda during his visit.

There was some progress the following year when the Scottish Minister for Transport, Infrastructure and Climate Change Stewart Stevenson was included in the UK delegation to COP 16 in Cancún, Mexico. He set out his priorities ahead of that visit informing the parliamentary committee ahead of the summit:

> Scotland has significant influence abroad and we are well placed to work with other countries to help persuade the EU and the international community that a global low carbon economy is feasible, affordable and indeed inevitable, and the sooner we make progress the sooner the world will reap the economic benefits.[117]

That work was built upon in the following years and gained further international recognition. In October 2011 Alex Salmond was awarded a prize given by South Australia every year for Climate Leadership. A previous recipient had been Arnold Schwarzenegger for his work when he was Governor of California. In one of his final acts as Premier, in fact on the day he stepped down, Mike Rann who later became Australian High Commissioner in London made the award to Alex Salmond praising the leadership he and Scotland had shown. He highlighted Scottish work on renewables, energy efficiency and the community engagement:

> Alex has been an extraordinary leader and just look at the examples that Scotland provides to the rest of us. Its commitment in 2009 to cut emissions by 42 per cent by 2020. Then to go further and cut them by 80 per cent by 2050, it's great to hear that already Scotland is half-way there towards its 2020 target... My government and so many governments around the world have worked closely with Scotland and we all admire Alex's leadership. So, congratulations to Alex Salmond for this year's award.[118]

The timing of the award could not have been better for the party and came as the SNP Conference opened.

Climate leadership was a key part of the Scottish Government's work as well as an important platform internationally. There was an economic and environmental domestic priority in tackling climate change, but it also allowed Scotland to engage with others from a diplomatic perspective. That was an important tool in foreign policy engagement when dealing with international leaders engaging in issues that sit within the remit of the Scottish Parliament. When signing the agreement with the Maldives in 2009, President Nasheed had made the case for action saying that there was a need for climate justice and that industrialised countries needed to help other countries who were facing the consequences of their earlier industrialisation saying: 'We are not seeking aid. We are seeking fairness.'[119]

In December 2011 Alex Salmond had spoken to the Chinese Communist Central Party School on the legacy of Adam Smith and climate justice. As well as giving the school a maquette of the 'father of capitalism', commissioned by the Scottish financier Sir Angus Grossart, he also became one of the first political leaders to talk about climate justice.

In a speech, drafted by Special Adviser Malcolm Fleming, who had joined the Scottish Government from the Oxfam campaigns team, Salmond brought together the teaching of Adam Smith and the Scottish Climate Change Act to make a powerful case for Scotland's international affairs agenda in this area:

> Those who have benefitted and still benefit from emissions in the form of on-going economic development and increased wealth, mainly in the industrialised countries of the west, have an ethical obligation to share benefits with those who are today suffering from the effects of these emissions, mainly vulnerable people in developing countries. People in developing countries must have access to opportunities to adapt to the impacts of climate change, and not be told to 'do as I say, not as I did' by the rich and powerful developed countries.[120]

He set out areas where Scotland was putting climate justice into practice such as its work with the Maldives on renewable marine energy and Malawi on solar power.

The reference to Adam Smith was quite deliberate, linking today's action on climate change to the Enlightenment in a speech that was given at the heart of Communist China. He also referred to another speech that had been made by the Chinese Premier at the University of Cambridge who quoted Adam Smith's *Theory of Moral Sentiments* where the Kirkcaldy economist wrote:

> if the fruits of a society's economic development cannot be shared by all, it is morally unsound and risky, as it is bound to jeopardise social stability.

The following year 2012 former UN Human Rights Commissioner Mary Robinson joined the First Minister in Edinburgh to launch Scotland's Climate Justice Fund, the first of its kind in the UK.[121] The Fund was praised by Mrs Robinson who said:

> Scotland is delivering on commitments to build the resilience of the world's poorest communities to the impacts of climate change. Importantly, delivering these commitments builds trust between developed and developing countries, who need to work together to solve the problem of climate change.

It won backing from NGOs as well with Judith Robertson, the head of Oxfam Scotland, who highlighted the implications:

> The Scottish Government has recognised that, in developing countries, the changing environment has a growing impact on some of the world's poorest people.

The mixing of climate action and economic opportunity was an important policy ambition for the Scottish Government. For example, in 2011 the SNP made a manifesto commitment to meet the equivalent of 100 per cent of Scotland's electricity needs (as part of the electricity mix) from renewables. This would mean that Scotland would continue to export electricity and critically that it would take the lead in terms of technology development.

That policy was described as a vision to re-industrialise Scotland and be a world leader in renewables. That was driven by the First Minister and with late nights at Bute House hammering out the policy. It was welcomed, again, by business, academics and campaign groups alike. That positioning as a global leader in climate change has been the right thing to do politically, diplomatically and economically with the World Wildlife Fund now estimating that not only has

Scotland met its targets but that it is 'sharing its renewable expertise with over 72 countries around the world'.[122] That is a powerful story of a green foreign policy agenda developed within the confines of the devolution settlement. A decade on both the renewables and climate targets are set to be met.

The figures for 2019 showed that Scotland's renewables electricity generated accounted for 90 per cent of the electricity it needed up from 27 per cent in a decade and well on course for 100 per cent.[123] Greenhouse gas emissions are down 45.4 per cent compared to the 1990 baseline.[124]

* * *

Scotland does not have powers in foreign policy, but these two examples illustrate that although reserved, and occasionally met with some hostility from the UK, Scotland has been able to pursue distinctive albeit limited foreign policy goals. It is not unique in pursuing foreign policy agenda, and it is worth looking at some other sub-state actors who are able to pursue their own interests in international affairs.

Across the world other sub-state actors with strong national or regional identities have pursued what is known as para-diplomacy. This has been described as the 'phenomenon of regional governments developing international relations'.[125] These usually have the consent and cooperation of the sovereign state with the rules for such engagement clearly set out in law.

This is clearly evident in Brussels where there are 300 sub-state representations who engage with the European Union. This is not indicative of foreign policy reach since the offices often deal exclusively with EU affairs including lobbying for regional funding and other work that is the direct responsibility of the local government entity. It does give an idea of the extent that sub-state actors are engaging beyond borders. Some of these actors have important powers.

Look North – The Faroes and Greenland

My geography teacher at Perth Academy, Mr MacLean, would invite first year pupils to look at the map of the world upside down. He would remind us that there was no right way up on a globe. We often think about the world around us via the prism of London and its neighbourhood. That sometimes makes sense not least with the shortest crossing to the rest of Europe and important access to the Single Market from Kent.

Scotland has long external borders to the north and historically we have had important relationships with near neighbours such as Iceland and Norway. Along our northern perimeter there are also powerful sub-state actors including the Faroe Islands and Greenland. They have significant powers and foreign policy clout developed in collaboration with the state apparatus in Copenhagen and set in law.

The Danish Foreign Ministry is clear about the relationship it has with Greenland and the Faroes. Helpfully it sets this out clearly on its website:

> The Faroe Islands and Greenland are part of the Kingdom of Denmark. As a main principle, the Danish Constitution stipulates that the foreign and security interests for all parts of the Kingdom of Denmark are the responsibility of the Danish Government.
>
> On issues such as security policy, European questions or the UN, there may, however, exist a strong interest among the Faroese and Greenlandic people regarding aspects of these policies. To safeguard the foreign policy interests of all parts of the Kingdom, a close and continuous co-operation exists between the Danish Government and Faroese and Greenlandic home rule governments.

The Danes are refreshingly open about the relationship stipulating next on the Foreign Ministry's website:

> Practice in recent years has shown a clear development in the direction of decisive Faroese and Greenlandic influence on matters of specific importance to the external relations of the Faroe Islands and Greenland.[126]

This collegiate approach is on display outside some Danish Embassies such as in London and Brussels where the Faroese and Greenlandic flags are flown alongside Denmark's flag. The crests are also up, Greenland's is easy to spot with a polar bear rampant.

The Faroe Islands sit between Scotland and Iceland and lay claim to the world's oldest parliament. The Faroese Parliament, originally called the *Althing* (its Parliament is now called the *Løgting)* was set up in around the year 900. That was around the time that settlers were arriving from Norway and shortly thereafter from Scotland and Ireland. The Faroes had an independence referendum in 1946, just after Iceland gained independence. There was a majority in favour but that was overturned after a parliamentary election. The Self-Governing Act of 1948 was brought in after that election, updated in 2005, giving the Faroese extensive self-rule.[127]

Under the Foreign Policy Act 2005 the Faroese authorities have powers to 'negotiate and conclude agreements under international law' on behalf of Denmark over areas where the Faroes have competence. Under this provision the Faroese authorities have negotiated free trade agreements with the EU, Norway, Switzerland and Turkey. They were also among the first who managed to sign an agreement with the UK after the EU Referendum having established a Brexit task group immediately after the vote in June 2016. The Faroes have even signed an extensive single economic agreement with Iceland, the Hoyvík Agreement, and signed fisheries deals with Norway, Russia, Greenland and Iceland as well as the EU.[128]

In a UK Parliament Foreign Affairs Committee evidence session ahead of the Scottish Independence Referendum one of the witnesses paid tribute to Faroese negotiating skills. Anthony Layden, a former British Ambassador and senior Foreign Office official, told the committee that during negotiations over the Continental Shelf Boundary the British negotiators found themselves being outfoxed by the Faroese:

> the Danes very cunningly devolved to the Faroese Administration responsibility for continental shelf matters. We found ourselves going to the *Løgting* in Tórshavn, which is wooden hut with a grass roof about half the size of this room, which was their Parliament. The Faroese simply would not negotiate with the British. They said: 'It's got to be a median line, it's got be a median line.' We negotiated very badly, and we finished up, after about seven years of talks, agreeing to a median line.[129]

The Faroese are active in several multi-lateral organisations including the Nordic Council of Ministers, the North Atlantic Marine Mammal Commission and are an associate member of several UN agencies. There is ambition to go further with the *Fámjin* Declaration signed in 2005 where the Danish agreed that the Faroes would be consulted over foreign and security issues.

Greenland has similar arrangements to those in the Faroes Islands. There is a slightly different focus given Greenland's own foreign policy priorities vary from those in Copenhagen and Tórshavn. Its own brief summary of its responsibilities is outlined by the Greenlandic Government on its website:

> The Department of Foreign Affairs main areas of responsibility are: Arctic co-operation, relationship with EU, UN and indigenous people's rights, Nordic co-operation, export/trade promotion and protocol.[130]

The focus for Greenland in international affairs is the Arctic and maritime issues for fairly obvious reasons given its geography. It regularly engages directly with UN agencies and ratified the UN Convention on the Law of the Sea in its own right after it had been signed by Denmark. Indigenous rights are incredibly important, and Greenland is responsible for continuous reporting direct to the International Labour Organisation, a UN agency, about the rights of indigenous and tribal peoples.

On the subject of defence, the Treaty between Denmark and the USA over the US Air Force base at Thule in Greenland, signed in 1951, was updated in 2004 to include Greenland. The Treaty is now described as an: 'An Agreement between the United States of America and the Government of the Kingdom of Denmark, including the Home Rule Government of Greenland.' There is an annual meeting between US, Danish and Greenlandic officials as part of that work.

Not everyone gets the niceties of devolved power – Donald Trump caused a diplomatic spat with Copenhagen and Nuuk by offering to buy Greenland from Denmark. The Prime Minister of Denmark had to remind him that: 'Greenland is not for sale. Greenland is not Danish. Greenland belongs to Greenland. I strongly hope that this is not meant seriously.'[131]

Copenhagen has signed agreements with the Faroes and Greenland clearly setting out the parameters in international affairs responsibilities, with Denmark committed to extending this where it is in the best interests of Greenland and the Faroes. It is also very willing to defend their autonomy in the international arena as illustrated in the exchange with former President Trump.

Across the world Greenland and the Faroes work with Denmark as well as undertaking their own work. Greenland has representations in Washington and Brussels with plans for one in Beijing. The Faroes also have representation in Brussels, London, Reykjavík and Moscow. The heads of mission are given diplomatic status by Denmark helping them in their work in the host country and enhancing cooperation between their respective officials.[132]

Both have a fascinating relationship with the EU. The Faroes never joined the European Union. Greenland left the in 1985 having joined as part of Denmark in 1973 before gaining Home Rule in 1979 and deciding to leave.

In the aftermath of Brexit, the case of a 'reverse Greenland' being negotiated for Scotland with Scots remaining and the rest of the UK leaving was suggested, although that was rejected by the UK Government. That could have been a means of compromise in 2016 for Remain-voting Scotland, Northern Ireland and Gibraltar. There could even now be some lessons that the UK could learn from the ways in which Denmark uses its sovereignty to build a more positive relationship and find solutions to tricky constitutional problems with the Faroes and Greenland.[133]

There is precedent in these islands where the Isle of Man and the Channel Islands sit outside the EU having never joined. In a submission to the Foreign Affairs Committee in 2016 the Isle of Man Government set out its concerns around Brexit since the UK is its voice in the EU. On the more general point around foreign policy the submission stated:

> In line with its constitutional status, the Isle of Man Government does not conduct what might be recognised as a formal foreign policy, but it does build relations with countries other than the UK, and welcomes the opportunity to promote economic, political, and cultural ties with other nations where possible.[134]

Jersey too has its own External Affairs Department that describes its work on its webpages as:

> We manage Jersey's external relationships with other countries and regional organisations, including constitutional, political, economic, cultural and environmental links. We hope to raise Jersey's positive international identity and Jersey's external influence.[135]

Jersey and the Isle of Man are smaller and more similar in population size to the Faroes or Greenland than Scotland but the precedent is an interesting one especially given the special status that Gibraltar and Northern Ireland now have with the European Union. Jersey takes care of its own Overseas Aid budget which is bigger than the Scottish Government's with a budget of £12.43 million in 2020 though of course smaller than that of Scottish taxpayers overall since its contribution is administered by the UK.[136] The same year Guernsey, with a population of 63,000, gave £3.1 million in aid.[137]

* * *

Sitting outside the EU is not a pre-requisite for having a powerful role as a sub-state actor as the hundreds of representations in Brussels illustrate. The most visible presence of all is perhaps that of Bavaria that sits in a stand-alone building, that some refer to as a castle, just outside the European Parliament. It is difficult to miss as well as being bigger and more prominent than some Member State EU missions.

Bavaria is not the only part of Germany with a large and well-resourced Representative Office in Brussels. The European quarter in the city is littered with the Representations of Germany's 16 *Länder* (federal states) that are powerful in their own right in EU and international affairs given Germany's federal constitution.

Anthony Salamone, who has written extensively on the subject and has provided evidence for the Scottish Parliament, told me that he was 'impressed' by the approach of the German states who 'aren't afraid of having a view even where they don't have competence'. This means they are part of the policy influencing process and some *Länder* have even had 'whole Cabinet meetings in the Berlaymont' (EU Commission Headquarters in Brussels).

Bavaria has a history of independence, different political parties from the rest of Germany and strong international brand recognition. The Bavarian state actively plays a role in seeking to shape and have an influence on European and broader foreign policy. Bavaria sees itself as very much part of the furniture in Brussels and this is reflected domestically where it has offered opinions on a wide range of international issues with EU affairs an integral part of the government's work. There is even a Bavarian medal for European integration.[138]

Germany's model of decentralisation and clear constitutional responsibilities helps this engagement. At the Committee of the Regions, the body that was set up by the Maastricht Treaty and provides a voice for local and regional authorities, politicians from around Europe gather. German representatives on the committee are often powerful politicians in Germany with a high national profile and influence.

There is strong intra-German collaboration between the *Länder* and the permanent representation in Brussels and at a Federal level in Berlin. The states have a good network of EU contacts and know-how built by years of hard work in the EU. Bavaria has also positioned itself as a bridge-builder between eastern and western Europe given its historic and geographic links. It maintains close links with its neighbours maintaining a special relationship with Austria, Switzerland and the Czech Republic. It even has a representative office in Prague and relationships with other states through the Association of Alpine states and the International Lake Constance Conference that draws members across borders. It maintains 28 trade offices throughout the world and 'hosts 43 diplomatic missions in greater Munich'.[139]

* * *

Just a short walk away from the 'Bavarian castle' and still at the heart of Europe is the Flemish Representation to the EU. It is one of several offices that the Flemish Government has established across the world. This one is closest to home since Brussels is the capital of Flanders, even though Brussels is its own federal entity and not part of Flanders administratively.

The Department of Foreign Affairs in Flanders takes an extensive approach to its work. It has a network of 12 representations spread across the world including Pretoria, New York and Geneva.

The Ministry website has details about its diplomatic links with international organisations and countries including trade information for just about every country on earth. You can look for trade and diplomatic information from Fiji to Finland at a state level and even on a 'regional' level from (Iraqi) Kurdistan to Macau on their informative website.[140]

The purpose of Flanders Foreign Ministry and policy is again clearly set out:

> Flanders is intertwined with its international environment. Some important challenges can only be tackled in an international context and by good cooperation with foreign partners. Therefore, it is a core task of the foreign policy of Flanders to defend the Flemish interests abroad. To that end, political relations in the EU, with governments abroad and in many international organizations are maintained.[141]

Within the EU it is important to be able to engage at a Member State level and the Flemish have it covered. That is important in influencing EU policy that is so important to Flanders especially when it has the opportunity to represent Belgium at the European Council where EU governments meet and the big decisions are made. Fishing for instance is exclusively a Flemish competence and so it takes the seat at European Council meetings and decisions on all fisheries issues since Wallonia and Brussels do not have a coastline. In recent Brexit negotiations the Flemish Government even took credit for a Brexit fund to help those most affected by the UK leaving the EU that was included in the European Union budget package that it claimed had been included in the EU budget 'at Flanders request'.[142] Flanders is an EU actor in its own right and one that the full Member States must take seriously.

This is a formal role that the Scottish Government can only dream of as the Brexit negotiations illustrated. Those restrictions have not been limited to the Conservative Government. In 2010 there were important EU talks on the future of fisheries policy organised by Spain. The talks took place the day before the UK General Election and the Scottish Fisheries Minister Richard Lochhead offered to represent the UK. Instead the Labour Government sent a member of the House of Lords who, although a Minister, did not have any responsibility for fisheries.[143] The devolved administrations have had to rely on the whim of the UK Minister when seeking a role at the EU Council. Some UK Ministers have been helpful, others less so.

The situation in Belgium is quite different where no level of government takes precedent over another in the pecking order. There is considered to be 'fundamental equality among all the governments in Belgium' without hierarchy and 'all Belgian governments are responsible for determining the federation's foreign policy'. Representatives of the sub-state entities, just like in Denmark, are put on the diplomatic list with the associated privileges.[144]

The Flemish Government also has representations to international agencies across the world and acts as a donor to organisations such as UNESCO and the World Food Programme. It has an extensive international development programme including humanitarian work and action on climate change. It also takes a foreign policy approach to defending human rights and in providing arms export licences – it will not provide a licence if the foreign buyer does not meet these criteria.[145] The Scottish Government does not have these powers and although Ministers may have called for a halt on arms sales, such as those to Saudi Arabia because of the war in Yemen, they have no power to stop such sales.

Critical to the success of Flanders and Bavaria has been the attitude of the Belgian and German federal state apparatus who see the work of the sub-state actors as complementing their work. Both the Member State and its composite parts benefit from the respect, clear guidelines and efforts of the other. In a European context that can be crucial as the Canadians found out when Wallonia blocked a free trade deal for a time between the EU and Canada by refusing to let Belgium, the Member State, sign the agreement.

* * *

It is not just in Europe where we find sub-state actors with a powerful role in shaping foreign policy and conducting international affairs. Elsewhere they can have a role such as the work undertaken by US and Australian states on climate change and other issues. In Canada the states have important roles, none more so than that of Québec which enjoys strong brand recognition and international links.

In 2017 the UK Foreign Affairs Committee travelled to Paris where we met with and spoke to parliamentarians including a joint meeting with our committee counterparts at the *Assemblée nationale*. At the end of the day we went to see the Europe Minister, Nathalie Loiseau at the Quai d'Orsay (French Foreign Ministry). Upon arrival we noticed that there was quite the ensemble at the entrance to the Foreign Ministry with a large reception committee, media in attendance and an honour guard along each side of the staircase wearing shiny breastplates and plumed helmets. We moved towards the entrance for what we presumed to be our welcome only to be ushered into a side door past the toilets and then up the stairs so that we didn't interrupt the honoured guest's arrival. The reception wasn't for us but rather a member of the Government of Québec who was in town.

Québec has always had an understandably special relationship with France. Over 50 years before our visit President de Gaulle had made a speech on the balcony of French speaking Montreal City Hall declaring *'Vive le Québec libre!'* causing quite the diplomatic stir with Canada and firing up the local sovereigntists.

Québec has continued to develop its own foreign policy footprint beyond France, though that relationship remains very important. In a recent study of sub-state actors' soft power by the British Council, Québec was ranked as having the highest score, with Scotland coming second ahead of Flanders, Catalonia and Puerto Rico among others.[146] The Government of Québec is very clear on this ambition stating that: 'Québec has its own specific role to play on the world stage.'[147] It goes on to list some of Québec's priorities:

- 'Make Québecers more prosperous by supporting companies', addressing tax and migration to benefit the economy;
- Contribute to a more sustainable, just and secure world' with a focus on climate, the north and Arctic, de-radicalisation and human rights;
- Promote creativity, culture, knowledge and Québec's specificity' though cultural exchanges and engagement in *La Francophonie*'.[148]

Canada's federal provinces have wide ranging powers and although foreign affairs is a federal competence the Government of Québec actively participates on a global level through its 'Ministry of International Affairs and La Francophonie'. It has a staff of about 475, with a budget of £67 million. In 2017 the department published its international policy 'Québec on the World Stage: Involved, Engaged Thriving' with its priorities including on the EU-Canada Trade Agreement (CETA) and northern and Arctic affairs.[149]

CETA has been particularly interesting since the Canadian Federal Government took the view that all of its provinces should be involved in the process and so secure their consent before and during negotiations by including them fully throughout. There were provincial delegates as part of the negotiating rounds too. As Anthony Salamone observed in his evidence to the Scottish Parliament:

> For the federal government, the implementation of CETA has been made easier by the fact that the provinces and territories were involved from the beginning and were on board with the agreement at the time of its signature.[150]

The province's engagement in *La Francophonie* is important for its links to other French speaking parts of the world. The organisation is not exclusive to French speaking countries, Ireland recently joined as an Observer at a meeting that was hosted in Yerevan, Armenia, another member. The organisation does promote the French language and links. Canada is a member separately from Québec. This provides an international forum to engage with states around the world that bring French speaking states and others who wish to be associated with them together. At a meeting to speak to the French Foreign Affairs Committee in Paris I noticed a large map of the world highlighting *La Francophonie* in their meeting room.

Overall critical to the success of these sub-state actors and their actions in the international arena is the relationship that they have with the state. There are clear rules and guidelines that are set out that clearly define the responsibilities of the sub-state entity and provide an outlet for any disputes or disagreements. That is more difficult where we have asymmetric devolution where the devolved administration is subordinate to the 'central legislature'.[151] Nowhere has that been more apparent than in Scotland and in the other devolved administrations during the negotiations about the UK's future relationship with the European Union during the Brexit process. The Scottish Government was even accused of 'undermining' the British position by engaging with the EU over devolved issues during the talks.[152]

The attitude appeared to be that even EU engagement was not the business of the Scottish Government. That is a position that is not sustainable. In a recent interview with the UK in a Changing Europe's Witness Archive, Philip Rycroft (who became Permanent Secretary at the Department for Exiting the European Union) said that there was some thinking by officials about keeping the devolved administrations involved. He describes the decision to trigger Article 50 without notifying the devolved administrations as putting 'two fingers up to them' saying:

> That drifted away from us, really pretty quickly. It was, perhaps, encapsulated around the time of the issuing of the Article 50 letter, which the devolved governments were told about 24 hours in advance. That was symbolically the moment when the UK Government, effectively, put two fingers up to them and said, 'We're deciding all of this without you in the room.' It's the UK Government's call. There's nothing unconstitutional about that. But if you want the evidence that in terms of the future of the United Kingdom, that might have been a mistake, we're now looking at opinion polls in Scotland where John Curtice will tell you that the shift, the tick upwards in support for independence, is statistically significant."[153]

CHAPTER 4

Scotland and the EU: An Unwanted Divorce

*For Ireland, our membership of the European Union and
our close working partnership with other member states,
has strengthened, rather than diminished, our
independence, self-confidence and security.*[154]

Simon Coveney, former Tánaiste of Ireland – *Global Ireland:
Ireland's Global Footprint to 2025*

COLLEGE GREEN IS a small patch of green grass opposite the Houses
of Parliament that provides a space for TV cameras to set up with
good views of Big Ben in the background. The morning after the EU
Referendum the world's media gathered on College Green to interview politicians and other commentators about the UK's decision to
leave the EU. At such moments the sense of drama and history on the
Green at the heart of the Westminster village can be overblown. No
one on that packed piece of grass in London that morning believed
that it was such a moment.

That morning's resignation of the Prime Minister was running
third on the news bulletins as we started to come to terms with
the enormity of what had happened. I had been on the overnight
media with responses to the vote counting as it came in. Speaking
to Brexiteers before we went on TV or radio in the first hours after
polls closed there was a sense from them that their side had done
well but fallen short. It soon became clear that was not the case and
the sense of shock was palpable.

The Remain camp hadn't fought a terribly good campaign. In
Scotland there was a recognition that the Project Fear playbook
doesn't work. The polls showed that the Leave campaign had less
ground to make up at the start of the campaign than the Yes campaign

did during Scotland's Referendum. There were also the years of press misinformation about the EU and the reluctance of successive governments to rebut those and embrace the EU. It was difficult to undo the damage of those decades misinformation about 'bendy bananas' and EU super-states in a matter of weeks.

No one knew on College Green that morning knew what was going to happen next. The UK Government hadn't prepared for a Leave vote and negligently neither had the Leave campaign, including senior members of the British Government. Boris Johnson and Michael Gove's press conference that morning certainly gave the impression that they didn't expect to win and had no idea what to do next. No wonder the pair looked so grim, shell shocked by what they had just done.

Four and a half years of crisis and chaos followed that have changed the UK and its relationship with the rest of Europe irretrievably. The story has yet to end but even with the last-minute deal on Christmas Eve 2020, just a week before the end of the transition period, it isn't looking good for the UK. The UK Treasury's own analysis, that MPs were only allowed to view in private while being supervised, painted a devastating picture for every sector. When I went to view the Treasury briefing in Whitehall offices just across the road from Parliament, I was given an hour and my phone was confiscated by officials when I signed in. However, the government research was clear – outside the EU we would see an economic downturn in every set of circumstances with the least worst option being the UK outside the EU but remaining a member of the Customs Union and Single Market. This man-made act of economic and diplomatic damage will be added to the mix over the coming years as the UK reels from the impact of the pandemic.

Joe Biden's Secretary of State (and Chief Foreign Policy adviser during his Presidential campaign), Anthony Blinken, put it succinctly when he described the UK leaving the EU as: 'the dog that caught the car and then the car goes into reverse and runs over the dog. It's a total mess.'[155]

The view from the rest of the world was not any better as the Brexit horror show continues to unfold. Truly a lesson in how to lose friends and influence while making a society worse off. The UK even rejected diplomatic status for the EU Ambassador and his team in the UK and so denying them normal diplomatic privileges under the Vienna Convention. An unnecessary and churlish slight on the UK's most important trading partner and a status afforded to the EU in the other 142 countries where the EU has representation. Even Donald Trump U-turned having made a similar move after just a few weeks but of course the damage was already done.

* * *

In Scotland we will face the same economic consequences even though the vote went very differently. The country voted overwhelmingly to remain in the EU. Sixty-two per cent was a resounding mandate and would have been considered a sizeable vote had any other Member State had an in/out referendum at that time. That was before Brexit made the EU even more popular in EU Member States than it had been before the crisis.

The result left Scotland (and Northern Ireland) at considerable odds with the rest of the UK. Every single one of Scotland's 32 local authority areas voted to Remain, including those who had voted against membership of the EEC in the 1970s.

The Scottish Remain vote was never a given, no vote ever is, but there has always been a pro-European sentiment that reached across the constitutional divide in Scotland. In the 2014 referendum the EU had been a factor with both sides arguing that EU membership was a positive either as part of the UK or with independence. The question of whether Scotland should be in the EU at all was very much a minority pursuit.

Throughout history Scotland has had close ties with its European partners. This has stepped up in recent years since the advent of devolution. As mentioned in Chapter 1, the Church of Scotland even felt comfortable in endorsing the EU in the Report of the Church and Nation Committee to the General Assembly in 1996.

Throughout the Church Report significant consideration was given to the future development of the EU with criticisms where appropriate and support for EU citizenship and further development of the institutions. There was an understanding and support for both concepts in some detail. The Church in the 1990s seems to have had a better grasp of the EU and its impact and makes a more intellectually robust interrogation of the EU than the UK Parliament managed

20 years later. The document is worth a read on its own providing fascinating insights:

> As long as the EU remains committed to an ever closer union between the peoples of Europe, transcending national barriers as an instrument for peace, justice, democracy and social cohesion throughout Europe and between Europe and the Third World, the Church should continue to support the development of the EU. That support is dependent, however, upon the Member States remaining true to the wider vision of the EU and not taking any steps which might turn it inwards to become either a 'rich man's club' or a 'fortress Europe'.[156]

This pro-European position has been re-endorsed by the Church again, including in 2014. David Bradwell who works at the Church told me that the General Assembly clearly felt that pro-Europeanism was a fair reflection of the broader Scottish society and that made the Church able make those kinds of statements in an uncontroversial fashion.

This engagement did not begin with devolution in 1999 but had been happening before and the Scottish Office actively engaged with the EU before then even under the Conservatives including throughout the 1990s. I spoke to Philip Rycroft, later the top civil servant at the Department for Leaving the European Union, about this. One of his early jobs was in Scottish Office Minister Lord Strathclyde's Private Office. The Minister dealt with fisheries and agriculture and was as Mr Rycroft explained 'very outward looking'. There was regular engagement with Europe, small EU unit within the Scottish Office and they worked well with the UK Permanent Representation to the EU. That was the 1990s however and he said of the period that it 'feels like the days of innocence'.

When the Scottish Parliament took over the Church of Scotland premises on the Mound in Edinburgh in 1999 those pro-European sentiments continued. In his speech at the opening of the Scottish Parliament Donald Dewar reflected on the impact Scotland and the Enlightenment had on the rest of Europe: 'The discourse of the Enlightenment, when Edinburgh and Glasgow were a light held to the intellectual life of Europe.'[157]

Scottish administrations and First Ministers have been resolutely pro-European ever since. To mark the 20th anniversary of the establishment of the Scottish Parliament there was a joint interview with Jack McConnell and Jim Wallace who served together as First Minister and Deputy First Minister. They highlighted the pro-European stance that they took in office and the active engagement in Brussels that Jack said he had been developing from his time as a councillor. He also credits former SNP MSP and Presiding Officer George Reid for his thinking around Europe in the discussions they had ahead of the re-establishment of the Parliament.

Speaking of his time as First Minister Jack McConnell said:

> We knew part of what worked in Brussels, where the networks were and that was why we set up the network of legislative regions. [Though he conceded he never liked the term 'regions'.] We knew we needed that network in order to influence the Member States.

To this day Scotland House brings together the Scottish Government, Scotland Europa and other Scottish organisations with excellent and well-used facilities at the heart of the EU district in Brussels.

In their joint interview Jack McConnell and Jim Wallace stressed the pro-migration approach that they had taken in office and its impact they believe it had on Scotland's decision to remain in the EU:

> We took a stand that was very different from most leaderships in Western Europe in welcoming immigration... And I think the result of that, partly, can be seen in the vote on Brexit in Scotland in 2016. I don't think the vote on Brexit in Scotland in 2016 had anything to do with European Structural Funds. I think it was about the national culture and the national culture had changed between about 2001 and about 2008 and it's been maintained since then. And I think we are a more liberal, more welcoming, more diverse place than we were back then.[158]

The SNP's win in 2007 resulted in an acceleration of that engagement with the rest of Europe. There was obviously a different slant with both SNP First Ministers, Alex Salmond and Nicola Sturgeon, seeing

Scotland's future as a Member State in its own right rather than as part of the UK.

The SNP is a strongly pro-European party as is the independence movement overall. There are some dissenting voices but these are very much in the minority. Brexit has galvanised support for independence and you will see plenty of EU flags at independence rallies and on social media pages. It is reflected in polling with the growth in support for Scotland regaining its sovereignty driven by Remain voters. The SNP Group at Westminster even got into trouble for whistling the European anthem, *Ode to Joy*, in the Chamber as we voted against leaving the EU. The whistling itself may have been out of tune musically and with parliamentary authorities but it was in tune with the people those MPs represented.

Over the years prominent SNP members have championed independence in Europe most memorably Winnie Ewing, known as *Mme Écosse* in the European Parliament. The late and much missed SNP parliamentarians Neil MacCormick and Alan Macartney also served in the European Parliament with distinction. All were great thinkers, parliamentarians and Europeans.

At Westminster the team of 56 in the 2015 parliament fought hard for Scotland to remain in the EU as did the MSPs although Alex Neil said he had voted Leave after the Referendum had taken place. SNP MPs were asked if they were comfortable with supporting the Remain campaign in a Group meeting by Angus Robertson and given the opportunity to come out for Leave, none did. Since then EU membership has become an important part of the independence arguments and cause.

It is fair to say that it was not always wholly the case. The SNP Leader in the 1970s and first SNP MP to be elected to Westminster at a General Election, Donald Stewart, referred to the EEC as a 'confidence trick' and campaigned against membership. He was concerned about handing over power to 'faceless European bureaucracy' and at the time represented a constituency, the Western Isles, that had voted against membership. Stewart felt more at home with the Commonwealth having served with Commonwealth troops and was the only leader at the time 'entitled to stand at the Cenotaph wearing wartime service medals', an opportunity denied to him by the Westminster authorities.[159]

That said, his parliamentary colleague Winnie Ewing was fiercely pro-European as were others in the group in the 1970s. In the introduction to her autobiography, *Stop the World*, Winnie wrote:

> We see an internationally minded Scotland, sitting where all the other free peoples of the world sit, sharing directly in our responsibility for this fragile planet and those who live on it and participating as of right in the European Union, United Nations and the Commonwealth.[160]

In his foreword to his father John MacCormick's book, *Flag in the Wind*, Neil MacCormick goes even further back to the foundation of the SNP. He writes of what he thought his father's attitude would have been when he wrote about the opening of the Scottish Parliament in 1999:

> I was deeply proud to attend that ceremonial opening as one of Scotland's then Members of the European Parliament. Dad would have been pleased too, for after 1958 he came to see that the European Community (now Union) was another theatre, additional to that of the Commonwealth, in which Scotland had a role to play.[161]

* * *

Even though the political consensus is now firmly pro-European in Scotland, there are real challenges to Scotland's interaction as the UK is struggling to handle that relationship. That is reflected in the debate and discussion around the internal market legislation and the post-Brexit relationships between the constituent parts of the UK. The Christmas Eve deal between the UK and EU was reached with very little engagement with the devolved administrations who were all against the deal, including the DUP in Northern Ireland.

Brexit has put significant strain on the relationship between Westminster and the devolved administrations. Henry McLeish the pro-EU former Labour First Minister who took over from Donald Dewar when he passed away in 2000, told me that 'Westminster puts up with devolution'. This has been seen beyond Brexit with a lack of understanding about devolved competences in dealing with the pandemic. During the early days of the Covid health emergency others spoke of Whitehall grasping devolution as Nicola Sturgeon led the response in Edinburgh and her counterparts in Cardiff and Belfast did the same working as equal partners to Boris Johnson in London.

'That is the sound of the penny dropping' was how one former Conservative Downing Street Adviser put it when journalists and others realised that devolution had real consequences. There was a sense of exasperation in the devolved administrations. The official Welsh Government twitter account simply tweeted '"national" = "England"' in response to Robert Peston stating that the Prime Minister would be announcing a 'national' lockdown after the devolved administrations had already acted in January 2021.[162]

This is not a new problem. Parts of Whitehall have found devolution challenging since 1999, not least when it comes to cooperation in Europe. A report by the Head of the Scottish Government Office in Brussels about Scotland in Europe was leaked to the press ahead of the Scottish parliamentary elections in 2007. The author, Michael Aron, a Foreign Office official, and currently the British Ambassador to Yemen, painted a picture of a devolved administration, then a Labour/ Liberal Democrat coalition, keen to be involved but being constrained at a UK level.

The report stated that Scottish Ministers were 'being held back from getting their point across where it matters in European institutions' and are kept 'out of the loop' and ignored by Whitehall. It said that Edinburgh would share information with Whitehall but not the other way around. In one case to do with whisky the UK Government had even acted against the industry's interests:

> The executive's access to the powerful group of Commissioners in Brussels is largely controlled by the Foreign Office, on condition Scotland argues the UK line. On drawing up regulations on spirit drinks, where Edinburgh was pushing the interests of the Scotch whisky industry, the report says the UK Government insisted on arguing the opposite case.

The report continued, that Scottish Government could be frozen out and the views of Scottish Ministers or officials simply ignored. It even refers to the Scottish administration being told about crucial meetings in London 'when it is too late to arrange travel and attend' and Scottish Ministers being sent to the *salle d'écoute* (listening room) when they went to crunch meetings in Brussels.[163]

These were damaging revelations of the way that Scotland was treated by the UK and it was all written when the two parties in power at Holyrood and Westminster came from the same party. The relationship didn't get much better after the SNP won the Scottish parliamentary elections a few months after those revelations in May 2007.

* * *

The question of independence has returned firmly to the top of the political agenda in Scotland with a firm focus on our relationship with the EU. However, the debate is confused by those who seek to compare membership of the EU as being similar to being part of the UK. Some of these arguments are down to political debate but others seem to be ignorance, wilful or otherwise, of the differing nature of them both. It is worth comparing these unions.

The false comparison between the EU and UK is often made by Brexiteers who do not wish to see the UK remaining in the EU but think that Scotland should stay in the UK. It is naive and shows a deep misunderstanding of how both the EU and UK work.

To be fair, a disinterest in the workings of the EU cuts across the political spectrum in the UK, especially prior to the vote to leave. In the run up to the referendum in June 2016 very few people turned up to the parliamentary debates on our relationship with Europe. It would often be the Europe Minister, David Lidington and Labour's Pat McFadden both of whom had an excellent grasp of the workings of the EU and some other pro-Europeans. I would speak in the debates for the SNP, usually joined by other SNP colleagues, and there would be an assorted selection of Brexiteers most of whom I recognised from watching the Maastricht rebellions on the TV growing up. They would turn up, tell everyone how awful the EU was, talk about its devious plans for taking over Europe, something about sovereignty and then perhaps round off with a story about the war or the Royal Family. That is a fairly generalised overview but one with some basis in the reality of the poor debate before the EU Referendum that certainly lacked scrutiny of the EU and none about what happened if the UK left.

It was disappointing but unsurprising to witness, in the years after the vote as Parliament ground to a halt, how little those who had campaigned to leave the EU knew about the subject and held on to their misconceptions. The UK's former judge at the European Court of Justice, David Edward, talked about the 'invincible ignorance' of Brexit backing Ministers and officials would complain about Ministers being unaware of even the simplest details about the EU.[164] As Foreign Secretary, Boris Johnson provided very little evidence that he had picked up any understanding of the EU or the single market since his time as a journalist in Brussels. Johnson spent five years in Brussels writing for the *Daily Telegraph* with one retired EU official saying of him: 'He was the paramount of exaggeration and distortion and lies.'[165]

There has been similar ignorance in those comparing the two unions. One of the major differences is most evident in the triggering of Article 50. The UK could decide to trigger Article 50 and leave at any time of its choosing, the UK never lost its sovereignty. The EU is a voluntary union based on the consent of Member States who agree the rules between themselves and can leave at any time subject to them giving the others two years notice. That was respected by the EU who worked with the UK to help deliver the UK's exit. The EU could never have blocked the UK leaving or the referendum and the UK could have held the referendum as often as it liked. There is no equivalent to Article 50 for the UK's constituent parts.

The question of sovereignty is clearly one that that still puzzles some in Westminster. In a taxpayer funded publicity campaign the Cabinet Office adverts referred to a future relationship with the EU 'based on friendly cooperation between sovereign equals'.[166] This has drawn criticism from around Europe.

In response to the UK Government campaign member of the Irish Parliament and former Chair of the Brexit Committee in the Upper Chamber Neale Richmond tweeted on 5 August 2020:

> Are the cabinet office saying that the 27 remaining Member States are not equals either to each other or to the UK? The Brexit delusion is reaching new peaks.

Former Conservative MEP Charles Tannock responded the next day:

> I too found the sovereignty emphasis language populist and v. 19th century. The EU is not sovereign anyway only its member states are as it derives its legal personality in international law from a Treaty between sovereign states who can withdraw from it when they wish as UK did!

It was not just the politicians, Professor Brigid Laffan, Director of the Global Governance Programme at the European University Institute in Florence tweeted:

> Please stop this 'sovereign equals' crap – who do you think you are fooling? EU not sovereign in the sense meant here. All 27 member states are sovereign equals within the Union. @cabinetofficeuk quit the propaganda – it actually undermines your country in the eyes of others.

It also made the rejection of diplomatic status for the EU all the more puzzling after the UK left the transition period. If the UK and EU were 'sovereign equals' then wouldn't they seek full diplomatic relations?

For those wanting to leave the EU it has been clear over the years that an idea of sovereignty lay at the heart of their arguments even if that came at other costs. Yet it is a fairly unique idea of sovereignty and one where the UK is now isolated with a different approach being pursued in the remaining 27 Member States. For those states sovereignty rests with the Member States who choose where to pool and share that sovereignty. That is particularly appealing to smaller Member States where 'the EU magnifies their powers beyond their wildest dreams'.[167] The UK has even gone further than Iceland and Norway both of whom are heavily integrated with the EU and even other EU neighbours leaving the UK uniquely isolated in Europe.

On a question of democracy, the EU has several checks and balances. The European Parliament is directly elected, the Commission, nominated by the elected governments and must be approved by the European Parliament. The European Council, that wields the real power, is made up of each of the governments of the independent and sovereign Member States. Each has a place around the table as equal partners ranging from Malta to Germany.

In the UK on the other hand the Upper House, the House of Lords is appointed. Many of the Brexiteers who criticised the lack of democracy in the EU now sit in the House of Lords and never have to face an election again. The elected devolved administrations can be over-ridden by the Westminster Parliament at any time. The EU (Withdrawal Agreement) Act 2020, a very significant piece of legislation with far reaching consequences across the UK and for devolution, passed even though all three devolved administrations withheld consent.

If there is a dispute between the EU Member States, they have the dispute resolution mechanism of the European Court of Justice. A state can take another to the court as can the European Commission if they think a country has breached its obligations. The court is made up of judges from each of the EU's Member States to uphold the agreements that those EU Members have made to each other.

There is no such mechanism in the UK. There has been criticism that a 'glaring gap in the UK's current system is the lack of satisfactory procedure for resolving conflict' where:

> disputes panels are chaired by a UK Government Minister, making it difficult for the devolved governments to have confidence that their cases would be considered fairly.[168]

Carwyn Jones, the former Welsh First Minister, remarked that this leaves the UK Government to mark its own homework in disputes.[169] Professor Anand Menon of the UK in a Changing Europe told me: 'You can't have independent trade policy and this devolution settlement.' This is even clearer with the internal market legislation and the agreement passed without the consent of the devolved administrations.

Over and above these differences is that European Member States have a veto on all EU trade agreements, EU budgets, constitutional treaty changes and a range of other areas including expansion. Penny Mourdant was wrong when she said the UK could not veto Turkish entry as a Member State.[170] I could go on highlighting where you simply cannot compare being in the EU and being part of the UK. One is a club for independent and sovereign states, the other isn't.

* * *

These differences around the EU go to the very heart of the emerging divergences between Scotland and England and how we fundamentally see ourselves in the world. As Scottish politicians and civic society understand EU membership is something that Scots sense. It was telling that only one of the 129 MSPs in the parliament that rose in 2016 just before the EU Referendum backed leaving the EU. Pollster John Curtice has said that it is driving support for independence and that 'Brexit has significantly changed the character of support for independence'.[171]

After the EU Referendum result there was even backing for Scotland to remain part of the Customs Union and Single Market from across the political and constitutional divide in the Scottish Parliament. There were offers of negotiation and compromise from the First Minister, ignored by the UK Government. In the House of Commons there were also MPs working for compromise with the SNP and others backing Nick Boles proposal of a 'Norway model' of leaving the EU. I spent a lot of time with Nick who was honestly looking for compromise and working with others to try and find a way through the stalemate. In the end he quit the Conservative Party in frustration over its intransigence acknowledging the willingness of the SNP and others to find a solution. He even crossed the floor sitting next to the SNP and Plaid Cymru on the Opposition benches criticising his own party's refusal to compromise.

During the EU Referendum it was often difficult to find a serious figure from politics or elsewhere to balance media panels and bring a pro-Brexit point of view in Scotland. That was reflected elsewhere in Europe where the UK decision resulted in a growth in pro-EU sentiment across Europe and support for the EU hit a massive 92 per cent in neighbouring Ireland for instance.[172]

In Scotland there is an acceptance of the need for multilateralism and the pooling and sharing of sovereignty with other states. Scotland will never be and has no aspirations to be a world power. It is different elsewhere in the UK with its commitment to a role with the FCDO's (the renamed Foreign, Commonwealth and Development Office) aspiration to *Global Britain*, an independent nuclear deterrent and as a permanent member of the

UN Security Council. There is also consensus around migration and freedom of movement north of the border. That acceptance of European norms and the rejection of British exceptionalism has been noticed by our partners.

In a speech to the Foreign Affairs Committee of France's National Assembly in Paris Nicola Sturgeon said:

> EU membership can amplify, not curtail, national sovereignty... for the Scottish Government, independence is not about the isolationism that characterises Brexit – instead independence would see us recognizing and embracing our interdependence with other nations. We will always seek to be close allies and partners with our neighbours in Europe.

To make her point she highlighted the position of Ireland and the EU compared to Scotland and the UK: 'the solidarity the EU has shown with Ireland since the EU Referendum, contrasts very sharply with the UK government's attitude to Scotland'.[173]

Her predecessor as SNP Leader and First Minister, Alex Salmond, summed up his feelings on the question of sovereignty when speaking at the Brookings Institute in April 2013:

> small countries often recognise that it is essential to pull sovereignty, but, of course, you have to have the sovereignty to pull. And the essential aspect is not whether you share or don't share, but whether you have the right to decide whether it's in your interest and the interest of your community to share sovereignty.[174]

The idea of working together and even that of sovereignty itself fits into the more pro-European tone that successive Scottish First Ministers have adopted. Anand Menon observed the importance of 'tone' and where Scotland could 'make itself distinctive to England'. It is important to adopt a message of 'humility versus hubris' when dealing with the EU he said. That can set you apart, language matters here and Menon suggested that Scotland should look at adopting a 'tone and style to differentiate itself from the British Government'. It is a good point and how you put your point across matters. It is worth remembering that the EU's effective working language is English, the words politicians in these islands say and report is heard and understood across the EU.

* * *

That pooling and sharing of sovereignty is largely supported in Holyrood and stands in contrast to the arguments that have come out of Westminster over the past five years. The policy divergences between the two were immediately apparent that morning on College Green.

Returning to the day after the Brexit Referendum, I was about to do another radio interview on the outcome when the interviews broke from the schedule and went live to the First Minister's response. As well as making comments about her disappointment at the result, importantly she also sought to reassure EU nationals by saying:

> I want to take the opportunity this morning to speak directly
> to citizens of other EU countries living here in Scotland – you
> remain welcome here, Scotland is your home and your con-
> tribution is valued.

It is easy to forget at such times the human element of decisions and that politics affects people. I have lost count of the number of EU nationals I spoke to in the years afterwards who remembered these words. It was important to them at a time when many EU nationals felt incredibly let down about the vote and uncertain about their future.

The First Minister stressed the importance of retaining links to the EU and that if taken out against its will this represented the 'material change of circumstances' that would lead to an independence referendum explicitly referred to in the manifesto on which the SNP had been re-elected in May, the month before the 2016 vote. She also highlighted the differences between the constituent parts of the UK and the EU Referendum result being:

> a sign of divergence between Scotland and large parts of the
> rest of the UK in how we see our place in the world.[175]

Since then the idea the Scottish Government has worked to retain the closest possible links with the rest of EU while the UK political leadership has sought what some referred to as a 'clean break'.

The UK Government complicated the negotiations and future relationship with its red lines around the four Freedoms, the European Court and other key parts of the European project.

As a consequence the Scottish Government has clear foreign policy objectives with Brexit representing a clear differential from that of the UK Government. Overnight the premise of any future independence debate and vote had also changed. Professor Phillips O'Brien of the School of International Relations at the University of St Andrews remarked of the change in circumstances from 2014:

> Foreign policy as a policy was incoherent during the 2014 referendum. Brexit, however, has given it an instant clarity and made it clear to many in Scotland why they now want independence.

The changes that we now know are coming were not clear at the time of the vote or in the immediate aftermath. The biggest single challenge for politicians since that time in London, Edinburgh or Brussels has been the lack of knowledge of what leaving the EU means. I remember one Tory MP, who voted to Leave, telling me, 'who am I to say what it means' and then Sky News reporter, Faisal Islam reporting the day after the vote that Brexiteers didn't have a plan but rather expected the UK Government to have had one.

That failure led to the years of stalemate in the UK caused by a lack of detail or even agreement from the referendum 'winners' on the post-EU model that the UK should follow. Even as late as 1 November 2017 Boris Johnson in his capacity as Foreign Secretary could not answer the question of whether or not he wanted the UK to remain in the Single Market when I questioned him direct about the issue as part of evidence to the Foreign Affairs Committee.

Christine Jardine, the Liberal Democrat MP and opponent of independence made the point that ahead of the Independence Referendum the SNP had at least published a 650-page White Paper. Brexiteers published nothing. There was no document to scrutinise and so no commitments to be kept. There was therefore a question mark over who had won the right to decide? That lack of detail led to the campaign for a second EU Referendum on the deal. We now know that the UK is pursuing a harder version of Brexit than even most of the Leave supporters envisioned as confirmed by the thin deal agreed between the UK and EU in December 2020.

What appears to have been at the heart of the Leave campaign and those who championed it in the House of Commons was the idea of parliamentary sovereignty. That took no account of devolution and the UK that left the EU in 2020 was not the same as had joined the EEC in 1973. A former parliamentary colleague close to UK Government's thinking told me: 'With a party founded on the premise of UK parliamentary sovereignty it becomes difficult to share that sovereignty.'

This will have long-term consequences for the future of the United Kingdom.

* * *

The Scottish Parliament has used the powers it does have to seek to retain close relations and alignment with the EU where it can. The Scottish Government introduced an EU Continuity Bill in June 2020 to maintain alignment with the EU on the environment and Scottish Ministers have been clear that they will seek proximity to EU rules where possible. Even back in 2016 the First Minister was telling the Arctic Circle Assembly that just as the Nordic countries have taken a different approach to the EU so too could the constituent parts of the UK.[176]

It is worth reflecting that within the Nordic states there are some who are in the EU, such as Sweden, others are not such as Iceland and Finland is in the Euro whereas the other Nordic states are not. The sub-state actors also have a variety of different relationships with each other and the EU with the Åland Islands in the EU, the Faroes never joined and Greenland left in 1985. One wonders if there are lessons to be learned from our near Nordic neighbours across the entities that make up the British Isles.

The Scottish Government rejected the UK's 'internal market' legislation as taking back control from Edinburgh as well as Brussels – as did the other devolved administrations. In August 2020 the Scottish Government published its initial assessment of the UK Government's proposals described as taking away powers from the Scottish Parliament on issues food regulation and buildings regulations among others. It described the UK Government proposals as introducing 'new constraints' on devolution.[177] These were done without the checks, balances and oversight that one would find in the European institutions.

The Scottish Government has retained regular contact with European partners and, as the First Minister told the French *Assemblée nationale*, doubled its trade representation in the rest of Europe between 2017 and 2019. That engagement has paid off allowing the Scottish Government to get its message across directly to an increasingly sympathetic European audience.

A significant part of the problem that the UK faces is the lack of formal structures to deal with the issues that have been thrown up between Westminster and the devolved administrations. Throughout my time in Parliament there was a sense, especially during the chaos of Theresa May's Government and after 2017, that the Constitution was outdated and at breaking point. Parliamentarians even had to go to court to allow them to sit after the unlawful prorogation. The rules may have befitted a 19th century club of gentlemen where decisions were made in one place and the monarch still had some kind of role but not a 21st century institution representing a multi-national state.

Throughout 2019 I was part of a cross-party group of MPs seeking to influence the Brexit outcome. At that point negotiations were focused on finding an agreement in Parliament. Some of us wanted to remain in the EU and others wanted either a softer Brexit or a more managed and coherent means of leaving the EU. In some ways parliamentarians coming together with key figures such as Keir Starmer, Oliver Letwin, Caroline Lucas, Dominic Grieve, Hillary Benn, Jo Swinson and others involved is how parliament is supposed to work. We were in regular contact through WhatsApp sharing information and drafts of legislation in a bid to find consensus. There was some success such as the European (Withdrawal) (Number 2) Act (or the Benn/Burr Act named after two of the other signatories) that stopped Brexit in its tracks on 31 October and prevented the UK leaving without a deal. It wasn't quite the constitutional change I might have wanted to co-sponsor but it did the job in the circumstances.

Ultimately those cross-party efforts were undone by the 2019 General Election and the Tory majority that was delivered. However, it was an insight into how parliamentarians could work together at time of crisis and in 2019 we managed to avoid a No Deal Brexit. It is telling that the Scottish Parliament has only ever had one majority administration and was able to operate effectively and pass legislation without a majority administration. Westminster on the other hand almost ground to a standstill when the Conservatives were just short of a majority between 2017 and 2019. A significant cultural shift is going to be required in the future since parliamentary majorities are not always guaranteed in elections regardless of the voting systems. At Westminster the winner takes all tradition where governing takes place with very little engagement and negotiations with opposition parties strikes me as being unsustainable. Between 2017–19 there was very little engagement by the Conservative UK Government with parties other than the DUP. On the other hand negotiation is necessarily an integral part of parliamentary life in Holyrood. John Swinney delivered all of his budgets in Scotland through negotiations when the SNP had just over a third of the seats (47 out of 129).

The breakdown in relations between the UK Government and the devolved administrations, exacerbated by Brexit, has left us in unchartered constitutional waters. The UK Government has shown its willingness to simply override convention and take policy forward regardless of the views of the devolved administrations. As the Public Administration Committee of the House of Commons found there is: 'growing consensus that the current UK inter-governmental relations mechanisms are not fit for purpose'.

Compromise will never be easy since there are different parties in power in Cardiff, Edinburgh, Belfast and London taking very different views on our relationship with the EU.[178] Although there has been some good cooperation in response to the pandemic there will be policy disputes in the future. At present the only resolution is that Westminster simply overrides the devolved bodies. That is unsustainable long-term.

Other states take a very different approach to the informal and centralised Westminster model. In countries such as Belgium, Canada, Germany, Italy and Spain there is a much more institutionalised method of working with set regulations between the state and their sub-state entities.

In the UK it is very informal with no such rules, relying on the goodwill of Westminster politicians. This might work when the same party is in power in both Holyrood and Westminster but not when there are different governments with contrasting political mandates. Henry McLeish once told me that when he had a problem with the Foreign Office or was needing to open doors he could phone Labour Foreign Secretary Robin Cook or other Ministers who were from the same party and with whom he had a long-standing relationship from his time at Westminster. It is difficult seeing Boris Johnson or Foreign Secretary Dominic Raab doing the same for Nicola Sturgeon or Welsh First Minister Mark Drakeford.

There appears to be little appetite to resolve this problem in London. One of the reasons the House of Lords has never been reformed is that it suits the government of the day to have a weak Upper Chamber with question marks over its legitimacy. The same is true for inter-institutional engagement with a Westminster that doesn't quite get devolution. As one constitutional expert told me that in terms of structures there is 'nothing there because the UK Government doesn't want there to be any structures'.

* * *

A former EU official who held senior positions in the European institutions once told me that the Better Together campaign were able roll out 'disobliging voices' towards the independence movement because those backing the campaign were well networked, certainly better than the Yes campaign. There were supportive voices on both sides, but it was clear that the UK was using its position as a Member State to influence other states. Most refused to speak out since independence is considered and remains an 'internal' issue. Member States are very reluctant to comment on the domestic affairs of other Member States. It was nevertheless a gap for independence campaigners.

Fabian Zuleeg of the European Policy Centre said that the pro-independence side could have done more before the referendum saying, 'in 2014 interaction with the EU was largely reactive rather than proactive' and that there had been a 'lack of engagement from Scotland'. He continued: 'There was very little understanding of Scotland's position in 2014 throughout the EU' and at times 'there was not enough done to counter any misconceptions'.

Since then attitudes in Brussels and Member State capitals have changed significantly. Brexit has been a 'game changer' in how

Scotland is considered and how it has been perceived since. Fabian Zuleeg added on Scottish engagement with the EU: 'That changed with Brexit and there has been a much more proactive approach at a high level from the First Minister downwards'.

In a recent paper Anthony Salamone wrote that the rest of Europe is paying attention to what is happening in Scotland:

> Scotland's opposition to Brexit – in particular its continued support for the free movement of people and its positive approach to EU citizens – has been widely noted by EU Member States. Its pro-Europeanism and the independence debate are the two main points about Scotland which actors in Brussels notice.[179]

This has been my experience from speaking to influencers across the EU. I travelled to Brussels and Member States during my time in Parliament meeting old colleagues and building fresh contacts. There was an interest in when Scotland was joining and an attitude of 'what's keeping you'? The conversation has changed since 2016 especially given the distrust that has built up between the EU and the UK, not least due to the hard-line approach taken to negotiations by the British and misinformation about the EU in the press and parliament. The repeated failure to understand, or even a desire to understand, the EU and how it operates has further damaged the relationship.

In the dozens of conversations I had with people across Europe for this book there was clearly an open-ness to Scotland joining as an independent Member State. One senior EU Commission official told me 'if there is to be an enlargement in the coming years, it will be Scotland' and that discussions in the institutions are that 'it is the only realistic enlargement'. An enlargement to the north or west is acceptable to the EU in a way that an enlargement to the east isn't just now.

David McAllister, the German Chair of the European Parliament's Foreign Affairs Committee, once tipped as a future German Chancellor said: 'Scotland at the moment has fulfilled the EU acquis to 100 per cent'.[180] In the interview with me, Mr McAllister, whose father was Scottish, praised the First Minister for her engagement in Brussels after the referendum while criticising 'the people who caused this mess... [they] were nowhere to be seen'.

I spoke to David as he travelled home from Brussels to Germany to discuss Scotland's foreign policy and its place in Europe. You can clearly hear that he learned his English from his dad growing up and has a distinctive accent. He told me 'Scotland is seen much more positively in the European Parliament, a lot of that is to do with the 62 per cent vote' and praised SNP MEP Alyn Smith's speech that won a standing ovation in the Chamber for Europe to 'leave a light on' for Scotland as 'one of the best speeches I have heard' in the European Parliament.

The European Parliament Foreign Affairs Chair did not share his view on independence and would consider that a matter for the people of Scotland. Nonetheless his insights were fascinating as an interested observer with strong personal links across the North Sea. He said that the German media use the terms 'Catalan separatists' but they don't use that term for Scots. It is more common to hear about those seeking independence or even nationalists when it comes to the case of Scotland. 'Separatist has certain connotations in German' he observed.

McAllister is not alone in considering the Scottish question among German politicians in Berlin and Brussels. The European Parliament's longest serving MEP and McAllister's predecessor as Chair of the Foreign Affairs Committee Elmar Brok referenced the Enlightenment and his time as a student in Scotland when he said:

> We need the Scottish people and their firm European beliefs. Scotland has shaped European civilisation, through iconic figures such as David Hume, Alexander Fleming and Adam Smith and still does so today by being at the forefront of defining and strengthening European values. We cannot afford to lose that... As a student I spent one year in Edinburgh. Since that time, Scotland is my big love. Due to this emotional bond I always have an open heart for the interests of Scotland.[181]

I met Elmar Brok along with other members of the Foreign Affairs Committee in 2016, his disdain for Brexit was clear as was his grasp of governing EU treaties that Member States had signed. The same could not be said for many of the MPs questioning him.

Supportive remarks for Scotland have also come from across the political spectrum in Germany. Gunther Krichbaum, Chair of the German Parliament's EU Affairs Committee, said 'the EU will continue to have 28 Member States, as I expect another independence referendum in Scotland'[182] just after the EU Referendum. Jürgen Hardt, the spokesman for the CDU/CSU Foreign Affairs group in the German Bundestag said there would be 'no high hurdles for Scotland to re-enter [the EU]'.[183]

Elsewhere in the EU there has also been support at the highest levels. In 2016 EU Commission President and Luxembourger Jean-Claude Juncker told a news conference in the aftermath of the Brexit Referendum that 'Scotland has won the right to be heard in Brussels'. Former Polish leader and EU Council President Donald Tusk told the BBC's Andrew Marr programme in February 2020 that the EU would be 'enthusiastic' if Scotland applied to join and for Tusk there was also an emotional link when he said: 'I feel I am Scots. I'm very Scottish now, especially after Brexit.'[184]

Even in Madrid politicians draw a distinction between the situation in Scotland and that of Catalonia. The former Spanish Foreign Minister under the right-wing People's Party, Alfonso Dastis has said that Spain would not attempt to stand in the way of an independent Scotland's membership of the EU. Asked directly by journalists whether Spain would veto an independent Scotland joining the EU, Dastis said: 'No, we wouldn't.'[185] That view was reaffirmed by Josep Borrel, Foreign Minister in the subsequent socialist Government in Madrid who said: 'If Westminster agrees, why should we be against it... I think the United Kingdom will split apart before Spain.'[186] Mr Borrel is now serving as the EU's Foreign Policy Chief.

In March 2017 I spent a day at the Spanish Parliament, *Cortes Generales*, and met with MPs from across the political spectrum with my colleague Emilie-Louise Purdie who was key to the SNP's approach to and understanding of the EU. It was clear that Brexit was important, though they had other priorities, but the faith in the UK had been dented in recent years. There was an openness to independence in Madrid if constitutional procedures were followed. That was also my experience in other EU Member State Parliaments.

No country would be more affected by Brexit or independence, outside the UK, than Ireland. I spoke to the former Chair of the Irish Senate's Brexit Committee, before his election to the Dáil, Neale Richmond. He and I had gotten to know one another well during the Brexit years where we would often find ourselves on the same side of television and radio panels. Neale certainly gave the Brexiteers a reality check on a regular basis. He also hosted Ian Blackford and I in Dublin when we held a series of talks with Ministers and TDs (Irish members of Parliament) from across the political spectrum in the Houses of the Oireachtas.[187]

Neale, who is seen as close to the Fine Gael leadership, told me that an independent Scotland could be good for Ireland. He said that 'Scotland would always be a key partner for Ireland' and that it 'would be a natural ally'. EU states find alliances between like-minded neighbours such as the Baltics and Nordics and elsewhere. He talked about the close partnership between Greece and Cyprus too saying, 'that's us and the Scots'.

Another newly elected TD, Cathal Crowe of Fianna Fáil, who is an old friend when we worked together in Brussels, was also supportive: 'Emotionally we in Ireland would love to see Scottish independence but it is not just emotions we see the economic benefits too' and talked about the close links that the two countries have forged. Looking ahead to the partnership and the isolation that Ireland feels from the rest of the EU geographically, now that the UK has left, Cathal Crowe added:

> In the Council of Ministers the UK didn't do us any favours
> but we have more commonality with Scotland and Ireland's
> main interests would align with Scotland.

Cathal's party leader and Taoiseach Micheál Martin has said that Scotland should be 'fast tracked back into the European Union if its votes for independence'. In the emergency session of the Dáil in the aftermath of the Brexit Referendum he told the Chamber:

> Scotland is strong enough to advocate for itself, but Ireland
> should be its friend and demand fair play should it seek to
> remain in the EU.[188]

Across the North Sea other neighbours are also paying attention.
Danish MP and former Minister Rasmus Helveg Peterson told me
that 'Scotland would be welcome in the EU and particularly as a
bridge-builder' with what remains of the UK and added:

> It would send a strong message that Scotland could and was
> willing to help mend relations and act as a bridge to the rest
> of the UK.

He also noted that although he expected the Scots and Irish to be
close, 'it makes sense that the Irish and the Scots would do the same
as the Nordics'. There were a lot of similarities with Denmark:

> You would automatically be aligned with the Danes on a lot
> of issues such as trade and climate change. You would be part
> of the club of liberal democracies like us. Scotland would fit
> right in with your own peculiarities.

On the question of the Euro and Scottish EU membership Rasmus
added:

> If Scotland didn't want to join the Euro and that was the
> single ask then that would be politically palatable but that
> would be a political question.

He did warn that 'there is a political price to pay if you are not
in the Eurogroup' referencing decision-making around the bailouts.
Denmark, of course, is not a member of the Euro, nor is neighbouring Sweden.

None of these politicians are advocating independence and are
keen to stress that it is not a matter for them, but it is a question that
is being given sympathetic thought across Europe. I spoke to a former MP who was spokesman on EU affairs in the Dutch Parliament
for the Prime Minister's VVD party, Anne Mulder. He said of Brexit,
'we are disappointed by it but we have other problems' and of the
debate in Scotland, yes, 'Scotland is a normal country' but it is not
'my focus' and that these are 'internal matters' for the UK. It is a

helpful and characteristically direct Dutch reality check. Europe is moving on from Brexit; the question is whether we move on with or without them.

* * *

The goodwill is all very well but the inescapable fact is that the UK has now left the European Union with a deal that would have been considered a very hard Brexit at the time of the EU Referendum. As a result, Scotland is now part of a third country in relation to the EU, a term that is used for countries that sit outside the bloc. That makes life more difficult and we must work harder for any influence.

The Scottish Government and First Minister have positioned Scotland well so far. From the day after the EU Referendum with the First Minister's clarity on the steps of Bute House to the present, the Holyrood administration have been clear that they wanted to maintain as close links as possible with the EU. The detailed work that has been done by Scottish Ministers and officials to prepare for the UK leaving the EU led by Michael Russell has been hard work diplomatically and bureaucratically but is important.

The Scottish Government has won praise from around the EU for its leadership, willingness to compromise and as one of the few voices in opposition to Brexit in the aftermath of the 2016 vote. In Brussels, Scotland House, led by senior official ex-Kinnock Cabinet member Mike Neilson, has been effective at working the Brussels networks without the resource or recognition of being a Member State. As MEP David McAllister noted: 'In the European Parliament Scotland House officials are very visible'.

It has managed to maintain a distinctive brand and identity that is important in the EU's crowded institutions and networks with 27 Member States, almost 300 'regions', businesses, NGOs, other assorted lobby groups, journalists and the highest number of diplomats in the world.[189]

The UK's credibility is incredibly diminished. In September 2019 the Belgian MEP and member of the Parliament's Brexit Steering Group Philippe Lambert gave the following interview to Matt Frei of Channel 4 News:

LAMBERT: There's no negotiations simply because the British position is to say we don't want the backstop and we don't want the backstop. Counter proposal, nothing. So basically, they say come back with something that pleases us. That's not a negotiation, so they are not negotiating.

FREI: So when he [Boris Johnson] is saying that there are tense negotiations going on and they are making progress, is that a lie?

LAMBERT: I think it's a lie. It's not because well you send a couple of people to Brussels to sip coffee together that you have negotiated. Negotiations is putting options on the table, negotiating the detail and trying to forge an agreement. He's not interested in an agreement, what he's interested in is giving the illusion that he negotiates in good faith with bad people and that ultimately if there's disorder, if there's disruption because of No Deal Brexit well you know I tried but these bloody Europeans can't really negotiate.

FREI: When you look at the politics in London are you filled with despair or hope at the moment?

LAMBERT: Well rather hope actually because there is clarification within the Tory Party, now we know that this has become an English Nationalist Party, a Brexit Party, not really better than Farage.

FREI: Is that the way you see it?

LAMBERT: Yeah, there's a clarification. English Nationalist Party. They claim to defend the United Kingdom in all its parts etc. This is rubbish they are English nationalist and they want Hard Brexit. They want No Deal Brexit to happen.[190]

What was so striking about this interview is that it is a fair reflection of conversations that I have had with colleagues across the European Union in Brussels and in the Member State capitals. Lamberts is saying in public what many are saying in private. That may have been before the deal, but the UK Government cannot wish away almost five years of ill will being built up with its nearest neighbours.

As part of the UK, Scotland has a challenge on its hands to maintain links. This will take resource and focus. To provide some context, Norway, albeit as a sovereign state with its own foreign policy budget, puts significant resources into engaging with the EU. The Norwegian Mission, just a couple of hundred metres from Scotland House, is its biggest in the world. Norway's universities, regions and other organisations have well-resourced offices in Brussels. The Norwegian Parliament even has its own office within the European Parliament, its political parties are members of European political groupings and its members interact regularly with their fellow politicians. There are particularly close relations with the other Nordic states, who share intelligence and information with Norway.[191] Brussels is important to Norway and Fabian Zuleeg told me: 'Countries such as Norway have usually sent their best people to Brussels.'

Scotland is in a position where it could act as a bridge to rebuild the shattered relationship between London and Brussels. Scotland's most important bilateral and multilateral relationships are in London and Brussels respectively. That will mean continued investment in our work with the EU growing the Scotland House model. It has been incredibly effective in its work, but the relationship will evolve quite dramatically in the next few years as the full impact of Brexit is felt.

I spoke to a number EU experts and those who work in the European institutions about what Scotland needs to do. They posed a number of challenges that Scotland should be setting itself on an ongoing basis. I have tried to capture some of the comments that I was given by senior EU policy-makers, decision makers and insiders in Brussels and domestically over the course of my conversations and interviews below:

1. **Strategy and Purpose** – There should be clarity on what Scotland House is for and its 'strategic purpose'. There will be a need for high level political engagement and in fairness Michael Russell understands that. Before the Covid crisis there had been plans for either Michael or his deputy Scottish Government Minister Jenny Gilruth to spend two days every month in Brussels. That would underline the

seriousness and importance that the Scottish administration places in its relationship with the EU.

2. The Expertise – One EU insider told me that the 'British system' has many strengths but one weakness is that it is a system of 'generalists' and so doesn't maintain long-term expertise in the EU. Senior staff members only spend a few years working on the EU before moving on. The rotation of staff means that the administration loses contacts and expertise that have been built up. It was suggested that the Scottish Government needs people with a 'deep understanding' of the EU and can't just send generalists. There are some with a lot of experience such as Mike Neilson but a relatively small number given the challenge. Some of the other comments I received underlined the challenges of maintaining effective engagement with the EU:

- 'The EU is a hugely complex machinery, you need to know the levers and the people, you need to be able to walk into offices and have serious conversations.'
- 'Scotland needs those with gravitas and their own networks in Brussels and at home.'
- 'You need those with political clout at home. Remember the EU has a hybrid model, so you don't just have politicians but some-one with a direct link to the levers at home and some 'political clout' in Scotland.'

3. Structure – Scotland House is considered to have done well in recent years to keep the Scottish Government and other organisa-tions engaged in the EU. It is made up of different organisations from across Scotland and is seen as so far having responded well to the ongoing Brexit crisis. It is those working at Scotland House who need to do much of the thinking around the future relationships so needs people with policy expertise including EU lawyers. They need to be fully connected to the Scottish Government's strategy and purpose and have a hand in developing that. There is an understanding that the new circumstances demand a fresh and strengthened approach. That will be difficult when resources are stretched so thinly finan-cially and bureaucratically.

Another consideration is identifying Scotland's key partners. References to the Hanseatic League, whom William Wallace was so keen to engage with when Scotland regained independence in 1296, have come back in fashion recently. The new Hanseatic League spearheaded by the Dutch, brings together the Baltic states of Estonia, Latvia and Lithuania along with the Nordic states, Finland, Denmark and Sweden as well as Ireland in the EU. The states reportedly meet regularly and work together especially around finance and – as a result of Brexit – will seek more common ground having worked with the UK in the past. One diplomat described the group as having the 'collective size of France with the competitiveness of Germany'.[192]

It is easy to see Scotland making common cause with such groupings depending on the issues at hand. As parliamentarians Neale Richmond of Ireland and Rasmus Helveg Petersen of Denmark agreed, Scotland could even help bring Ireland closer to these groups including the Nordic states given our connections. That will be helped by targeting resources at key partners and there are advance plans by the Scottish Government to open a new Scotland House in Copenhagen strengthening links with the Nordic and Baltic states.

This will require further investment when budgets are stretched due to the economic crisis caused by Covid-19 and Brexit. There will also need to be other imaginative, less-costly ways in which to engage. States work hard to get their key people into EU Cabinet posts (a Cabinet is the office of a Commissioner). This is something that has been done in the past. Philip Rycroft talks of being 'tapped on the shoulder' to work in Leon Brittan's Cabinet, when he was Commissioner, having been seconded from the Scottish Office. Philip readily admits that it was a European post, but he did seek to 'operate in Scotland's interests' when there was an opportunity. That may be difficult now given that there are fewer UK officials in the EU institutions. Here there could be a role for the diaspora in the EU to play both in the institutions and Member States. There are still plenty of Scottish officials left in the EU, many in influential posts, who are keen to help.

Scotland's cross-party pro-EU attitudes will help connections but will not be enough over these next challenging few years. There will need to be a national conversation ongoing on how we continue to maintain this links. This cannot simply be left up to the government. All organisations have a role to play as many do in Scotland House already.

Our Universities for example have an outsized opportunity to make a difference. David McAllister said:

> Beyond the official levels the Scots can reach out, the Scottish universities in particular have a role to play. Many EU officials send their children to Scottish universities.

Across the world, including Brussels, there are MEPs, officials and others who have either gone to a Scottish university or sent their children. The Scottish Government has recently had to change the rules around fees due to Brexit which will have an impact on poorer but gifted students who previously came to Scotland.

There is no immediate way around that damage, but one can seek to minimise it such as using the finance for scholarships previously used for EU students to attract talented students who would not otherwise been able to afford to come. That could be for instance with a scholarship say named after a great Scot such as Duns Scotus, Jane Haining, Adam Smith or David Hume. Scotland's educational links with the rest of Europe run deep and there will be a concerted effort required to maintain those. This could be especially important at a diplomatic level since Scotland's Higher Education sector is genuinely world-leading and an area where EU members will see the benefit of cooperating with the Scots. It is an asset that Scotland brings to the EU table, along with expertise in renewable energy for instance.

Limited finance and limited diplomatic reach, as a part of a third country, will be significant challenges for Scotland. That means difficult decisions and enhanced engagement where possible. The UK has left the EU and that means Scotland has left too. That changes the way in which the EU, UK and Scotland interact with one another. During a meeting I had with Michel Barnier he remarked that the moment the UK left the EU, or the Single Market for that matter, the EU changed, 'an EU of 27 is not the same as an EU of 28'. There isn't simply a UK shaped hole to be filled and it is a different creature now to the one the UK left.

As well as changing the rules when we interact with the EU so too Scotland's relationship with the rest of the UK will change if we re-join. Kirsty Hughes, who founded the Scottish Centre on European Relations, has highlighted the question of the border with England that will have to be considered as part of any independence debate as the relationship between the UK and the EU at last becomes clearer.[193] It is a point worth considering. Even though many of us think the Brexit project is fundamentally a bad idea that will be damaging it is a reality that must be dealt with. Scotland's relationship with the rest of the UK including a shared land border will be a key part of EU accession. If done right the border could help bring what remains of the UK and the EU closer together again in the future but remains a challenge. The deal between the UK and the EU provides the building blocks but will need to be worked up in greater detail.

Scotland has the political goodwill and many of the institutional structures to become an EU Member State but there is still plenty of work to be done to fulfil that aspiration. As one EU expert close to the Better Together campaign mentioned to me, 'it isn't a huge leap of imagination for Scotland to be seen as a full Member State'. The official referenced the OECD where you see Ireland, Denmark, Finland and other medium-sized European states doing well and that Scotland is a 'natural fit'. That is encouraging but not enough though and all these positives for Scotland do not negate the damage of Brexit and the changes that has brought.

You could sense former First Minister Henry McLeish's frustration when he told *The National* that: 'We can't hang around and wait for the triple challenge to Scotland of a health pandemic, an economic recession and a No-deal Brexit,' as he called for First Minister Sturgeon to negotiate a Scotland-only Brexit extension.[194]

He told me: 'Scotland needs to be careful not to tie itself to the UK's broken system.' We must be realistic about what is possible given the limited powers that Scotland has and the reluctance of the UK Government to cooperate with the Scottish Government on the matter.

Regardless, the engagement must go on at a high level and in a meaningful way. Professor Nicola McEwen put it this way: 'small states invest heavily in networking, and using soft power to persuade, to generate new ideas'. In other words, we should learn from others and keep up the engagement and the message that Scotland wants to join. Michael Russell and the Scottish Government get that and as Russell told me there is a 'helluva a lot to be learned from the Irish'. It helps that, as David McAllister pointed out, English will remain the working language of the institutions and having another English-speaking country in there would be welcomed.

Former Scotland Office Minister Lord Ian Duncan and I worked together at Scotland House before either of us went into politics remarked to me: 'The game has changed, and Brexit has done that'. We just don't know the outcome yet.

CHAPTER 5

The Other Neighbours: Scotland and the High North

*Iceland is... as hoachin with gingers as
Sauchiehall Street.*[195]

Alastair Heather, *The Scotsman*, 17 May 2020

HANS ISLAND IS a small uninhabited island sitting in the Nares strait between Canada and Greenland. It sits within 12-mile territorial limit of Danish and Canadian waters and is claimed by both. A 1973 treaty between the two countries couldn't decide what to do about the island, so a decision was deferred. The way that Copenhagen and Ottawa have dealt with the dispute is unusual in a world where all too often confrontational rhetoric or worse would be the normal recourse.

In 1984, Canadian troops visited the island leaving a flag and a bottle of Canadian whisky. Tensions escalated when a Danish Minister returned with a bottle of Danish schnapps and a note: 'Welcome to the Danish Island'.

Both have a serious territorial claim, but they do not let that get in the way of good neighbourly relations. For the Nordics and Canadians, the rule of law and maintaining peaceful relations are more important than forcing a resolution on this territorial dispute.[196]

Recently Scotland has had its own territorial dispute with Ireland over the status of Rockall and access to its rich fishing grounds. In many ways this is a slightly trickier situation than that with Hans Island, but the leaders of Scotland and Ireland have stressed that they will seek to work on finding a solution. After talks with First Minister Sturgeon, then Taoiseach Leo Varadker said, 'we want to be united on Brexit and not falling out over issues such as Rockall'.[197] No one has yet left a bottle of spirits on the rocky outcrop so we are yet to witness a war of words over whether whisky or whiskey has been left to mark the island's status.

There is a serious point here that respect for the rules-based system and good neighbourly relations are more important to these states than other advantages that might be gained from seizing the island. Nordic states have built global reputations and international clout on that basis. In a speech on Scotland's soft power and foreign policy potential, Mark Muller Stuart QC remarked upon the lessons that we had to learn from our neighbours as well as the similarities noting:

> most people from small northern European states tend to support the use of soft rather than hard power to resolve conflict in international affairs.[198]

* * *

Scotland's links with and similarities to its Nordic neighbours goes way beyond how we deal with territorial disputes. There have been strong historic links between Scotland and these countries going back to the very foundations of our respective nations. Political marriages were arranged between Scottish and Nordic monarchs, James VI married Queen Anne of Denmark for example before the Union of the Crowns in 1589, and there are strong links through migration, in both directions, throughout the centuries. Some even argue that Scotland should be considered a Nordic country rather than simply a neighbour.

Across Scotland there are signs of these connections with place names and cultural events such as the annual Up Hellya Aa festival that takes place every January in Shetland. Sutherland on mainland Scotland is so named because it was Southland in Old Norse and elsewhere strong Nordic links remain.

There are strong links in the Nordics too. The Swedish army had thousands of Scots serving throughout the centuries, the industrial revolution made it to Finland via Scotland and Iceland's first population is said to have had a big proportion of Scots, about two-thirds of the women.[199]

You can even see the links today among Scotland's gingers whose hair colour is said to have arrived in Scotland via our Viking ancestors. Just 0.6 per cent of the world's population has red hair compared to 13 per cent of Scots. Professor Donna Heddle of the University of the Highlands and Islands told *The Scotsman*:

> The only other density of red hair which compares to Scotland and Ireland is in Scandinavia. It becomes a cultural marker of the Norse and of the Vikings. If you look at where the red-haired patterning is in Ireland, in particular, it is very much around the areas where Vikings settled.[200]

Others disagree and say that the gingers were already here and that the Vikings just brought another variation of the gene. Either way there is clearly a connection that goes both ways as it does with neighbours anywhere.

Mariot Leslie, a former British Ambassador in Oslo said, 'Norway would want to regard Scotland as close friends, virtually kith and kin'. Danish MP Rasmus Helveg Petersen also said that the Scots would be close to Denmark – 'Scotland would fit right in with your own peculiarities'. Ulf Bjereld, a Swedish political analyst with close links to the Social Democrats said it was a pity Scotland hadn't voted for independence after the 2014 vote: 'I think there's a certain weakness for Scotland in Sweden. We look at it as the Nordic part of Great Britain.' Though others, such as former Prime Minister Carl Bildt, did welcome the No vote at the time – it was support for the stability of the status quo.[201]

Both sides continue to build on those links. The day before the UK formally left the EU, 30 January 2020, a delegation from the Presidency of the Nordic Council visited the Scottish Parliament where the President, Silja Dögg Gunnarsdóttir, told her hosts:

> Historically there have always been close ties between the Nordic countries, Scotland and the rest of Britain. The Nordic Council will do everything in its power to ensure that this close cooperation continues. Despite Brexit, we want Scotland to know that she will always have friends in the Nordic countries.[202]

Those links are strong and will remain so with a relationship that has been formed distinctively with and by Scotland rather than simply a part of the United Kingdom.

* * *

The SNP has long taken an interest in the Nordic Council with members of the party, such as former Westminster leader Angus Robertson, arguing that Scotland should consider joining. The Scottish Government White Paper that was published ahead of the Independence Referendum in 2013 stated:

> The Government intends that Scotland will also seek a closer relationship with the Nordic Council of Ministers. Scotland has key shared interests with our geographical neighbours in the North Atlantic, such as Iceland and Norway, and a common interest in the Arctic and High North.

The Nordic Council provides a forum for cooperation between the Danish, Icelandic, Norwegian, Swedish and Finnish states as well as the Faroes, Greenland and the Åland islands. Recently it has focused on sustainability and climate change given the close environmental links between the members for whom this is a political priority. Like Scotland they have taken a leading global role in tackling climate change.

Each member of the Nordic Council is either independent and sovereign or carries a high degree of autonomy. Of the autonomous members only the Åland islands is part of the EU. Even then it had to consent to joining, under its Autonomy Act, and could have remained outside of the EU if it had chosen to do so even though Finland is a member.[203] Under its special status, for those who like a good deal, you can get 'duty free' when travelling from the islands to another part of the EU.

Each member in this family of nations maintains their distinct identity. The Danish academic Bjarke Dreyer wrote in *The National* in February 2020 that Scotland should 'come back' to Scandinavia and join the Nordic Council. In doing so he set out how the Nordics see themselves:

> In the Nordic countries we are proud of our national identities. We are Danish, Swedish, Finnish, Norwegian, Icelandic, Greenlandic, Faroese and *Åland* Islander first, and Nordic second, and European third. We are sibling countries, but each of us forge our own path. When we meet out in the wider world, we feel a real sense of kinship. Perhaps one day we could add Scottish to that list.[204]

There appears to be some open-ness about Scottish membership. We have already seen that the Finnish newspaper *Helsingin Sanomat* argued that Scotland should be considered 'The Sixth Nordic Country'. The newspaper highlights that, when it achieved independence, Finland was not assumed to be part of the club having just won its independence from Russia and to this day considers itself a Nordic rather than a Scandinavian country.[205]

When I spoke to Rasmus Helveg Petersen, he was not against the idea though he did highlight this:

> The Nordic Council is culturally very important to us but politically of little importance. Many of the Nordic Council's achievements have been overtaken by the EU.

That makes sense and makes Scottish interaction with the Nordic Council more straight forward given it is built on commonality and informal links. It is easy to see how the Nordic Council could be a way for Scotland to maintain and build upon links with our neighbours to the north and east outside or within the EU. This need not always focus on the relationship with government in Edinburgh and it is easy to see Nordic Council meetings and other events taking place in Lerwick and Kirkwall for instance.

* * *

Like other northern countries the Scottish Government is addressing areas it can work with neighbours in the Arctic. Global warming means that the Arctic is becoming more accessible to transport and commerce due to melting ice bringing, economic and security challenges and opportunities.

The Scottish Government appears to paying closer attention to the Arctic than the UK Government. That is natural given geography but there has been some criticism at Westminster that the UK Government has failed to take the issue as seriously as it should with concerns expressed by committees in the Lords and Commons recently.[206] A Commons Defence Committee Report criticised the UK for failing to appoint an Arctic Ambassador and repeated 'concerns voiced by the House of Lords Arctic Committee about the way in which UK Arctic policy is prioritised and co-ordinated.'

In 2011 Angus Robertson, then SNP Westminster leader, argued that 'the UK has opted out of taking a serious approach to the economic and military changes the melting ice cap will bring' when the 2010 Strategic Defence and Security Review failed to mention the Arctic.[207]

More recently, the Scottish Government published 'Arctic Connections: Scotland's Arctic Policy Framework' in September 2019. The focus of that document was very much on devolved areas of responsibility. The External Affairs Minister Fiona Hyslop highlighted that the framework was about the areas where the Scottish Government had devolved responsibility. The framework focused on issues of common concern in a bid to position Scotland as the:

> European gateway to the Arctic and establishing it as the international partner of choice for both our Arctic neighbours and other like-minded countries.[208]

The Scottish Government's framework won praise for that work and Dan Kenealy of the University of Edinburgh described the difference between the UK and Scottish Governments' work on the Arctic as being 'night and day'.

The Scottish Government has had to take a different tack on the Arctic from the UK. It cannot simply ignore the issue given its economic potential, and associated challenges. The 2010 UK Strategy Review had not even mentioned Scotland let alone consulted the Scottish Government. Former British Ambassador to Iceland and much missed, Alyson Bailes, who advocated stronger Scottish involvement in the north, criticised the UK Government in 2013 for publishing its strategy 'late to the game' and 'without referring to any special or separate interests of Scotland, Wales or Northern Ireland'.[209]

Scotland is not the only sub-state actor to adopt an Arctic policy, others such as the Faroes and Québec have also done so. It provides a good example of where Scotland can engage in an area of international affairs with its neighbours, with whom, it has a special relationship due to history, geography and policy that doesn't exist elsewhere in the UK. That interaction is gaining traction with the organisation, the Arctic Circle even coming to Edinburgh in 2017 in recognition of 'a northern country with a long history of Arctic commercial endeavour, exploration, and scientific research'.[210] The Arctic

Circle describes itself as a network for dialogue and cooperation on the Arctic bringing together governments, companies, universities, think tanks and indigenous communities among others.[211]

This is an area where the Foreign Office has had different priorities from Scotland and the Scottish Government has stepped up. Devolution does bring its limitations, but the Scottish Government Arctic Strategy is focused on using existing powers. It is easy to see where the Foreign Office could have benefitted from greater cooperation with the Scottish Government and even other devolved administrations.

There is scope for an even more 'regionalised' approach with Alyson Bailes suggesting 'West Nordic' cooperation with our neighbours in Iceland, Greenland and the Faroes on 'cultural and social projects'.[212] Those three already cooperate and on 23 September 2020 the three flags flew outside the Faroese Parliament to mark 'West Nordic Day'.

The Scottish Government is ambitious in its Arctic policy and rightly so. Their aim to become a European gateway to the Arctic is the kind of positioning that the government needs to take in a post-Brexit world. When the UK Government is closing doors with Europe the Scottish Government should be about opening them up again. This was the take of the Norway-based *High North News* when reporting on the Scottish Government strategy:

> Another reason is Brexit, which creates great uncertainty both inside and outside the UK. The Brexit process in the UK has met strong opposition in Scotland. The referendum showed a strong support for 'remain' in all Scottish electoral regions. Even if the final outcome of Brexit is not clear at the moment, establishing stronger ties towards the North, especially the Nordic countries and the North Atlantic region, can be seen as a strategy to open up other doors.[213]

* * *

These connections are helpful and help maintain relationships with our near neighbours. The Arctic is just one part of the relationship and important as it is Professor Malcolm Chalmers of RUSI (Royal United Services Institute) argued: 'The North Sea/North Atlantic area will be more important than the High North'. He may be correct, but the Arctic strategy is a good one to consider in terms of building for the future and an area we need to consider in terms of Scotland's foreign policy.

Among our neighbours there is shared outlook in policy, geography and world view. Those links go beyond politics and diplomacy. During a visit to Scotland in 2013 the Danish actress Sidse Knudsen, who played the Prime Minister in the TV series *Borgen*, said that she felt at home in Scotland:

> I kept on hearing what I thought were Danish people. I had to listen again before I realised it was just Scottish people chatting away – for a moment it felt like I was back home.

Anyone who has visited the Netherlands, Denmark or Norway will automatically see a link between the languages spoken there and in Scotland.[214] As a student in Antwerp my grandfather, with his Dundonian accent, called me for a chat one evening. He asked my Austrian friend if he could speak to me and after the two tried to understand one another my flatmate had to ask him if 'he spoke English since his Dutch wasn't so good'.

Sounding similar isn't foreign policy but it is fair to say that over the course of this research it has been easy to see evidence of that commonality among our neighbours in the northern North Sea and North Atlantic region.

In 2006, SNP Leader Alex Salmond argued that Scotland should join an 'arc of prosperity' of its successful near neighbours, Ireland, Iceland and Norway. He was criticised at the time with opponents later describing it as an 'arc of insolvency' during the banking crisis.[215] I have always thought that criticism was somewhat short-sighted not least given the fact that these countries continue to outstrip UK economic performance.

This is not a book about the economy but surely if your neighbours are outperforming you, it is a pretty good place to start looking for ideas. Reports regularly have Scotland's similar sized neighbours at the top of economic and quality of life performance indicators. They must be doing something right that those who talked about an 'arc of insolvency' are not.

Fortunately, Scots have not been put off and it has been good to see those involved in politics look elsewhere for ideas. Broadcaster Lesley Riddoch has released a series of films on lessons we can learn from these neighbours. The baby box was a classic idea that the SNP openly took from Finland for its 2016 manifesto and in 2020 an Irish Fine Gael TD said that the introduction of the baby box to Ireland by its new government came to Ireland from Finland via Scotland.[216]

It is a good example of where commonality of politics and world view is important in building alliances and relationships. It has driven the EU together over the past 70 years and is now driving a wedge in the UK with very different foreign policy outlooks emerging among the political classes and the people they serve in parliaments in London and Edinburgh. Our neighbours were as horrified as many Scots when the Northern Ireland Secretary, Brandon Lewis, told the House of Commons on 8 September 2020 that the UK Government's plans for its internal market legislation broke international law, telling the House: 'Yes, this does break international law in a very specific and limited way.'

The idea of the rule of law and respect for international law is incredibly important to our allies in the north. Multilateralism and a respect for the rules-based system sits at the heart of their foreign policy. They believed that was also the case with the UK and the damage of remarks like Brandon Lewis' can take decades to undo. That is why events in London recently undoing that post-war consensus is so horrifying to many of our neighbours and damaged the UK's standing amongst its closest allies. The closeness between pro-Brexit politicians such as Boris Johnson and Nigel Farage was seen as part of that pattern including the links that they had to Donald Trump's administration.

Foreign policy is driven by domestic priorities, politics and how we see ourselves. It is easy to see why we have so much in common with Nordic and Baltic neighbours and why that cooperation should be strengthened. That needs to find a relevance and foundation domestically, after all the most important driver in international affairs is domestic politics.

An international affairs analyst once told me that she had attended a speech by Nicola Sturgeon on foreign policy at the

University of Georgetown in Washington DC. She delivered a thoughtful speech tackling the big international affairs of the day. Afterwards in one of the first questions, the First Minister was asked about speed bumps on the Nithsdale Road in her Glasgow Southside constituency.

These relationships with our Nordic neighbours were underpinned by our membership of the European Union in the recent past. Maintaining that requires greater imagination now that Scotland is part of a third country in relation to the EU and its Member States and so does not have the same access to the institutions. Even within the Nordic Council, the EU is becoming a more important means of cooperation for the states even those who are not EU Members.

In September 2017 the Scottish Government published its strategy for working with Scotland's Nordic and Baltic neighbours. This focused on areas of domestic policy where there was common ground to build collaboration. The Baltics work closely with their Nordic neighbours and there is a desire for more cooperation. The Scottish Government's All Points North policy statement referred to this:

> Scotland is a country with a strong reputation as an outward-facing European nation. From our location in the northwest corner of the continent, we have always looked outwards building strong cultural, economic and social links with our neighbours across the continent.
>
> This is especially the case with our Nordic and Baltic neighbours where historic and contemporary connections continue to shape the lives of citizens in our countries.[217]

The statement highlighted areas where Scotland enjoys leadership and where Scotland wants to work more closely with our neighbours in areas such as 'low carbon economy, healthcare, sustainability, closing the attainment gap, social policy, digital etc'. Policy areas where we can learn from each other, have common challenges and a degree of policy alignment. The First Minister highlighted this work in her speech to the Arctic Forum in Edinburgh and includes:

- joint work with the Icelandic tourist authorities on sustainable tourism;
- learning from Denmark on cycling infrastructure;
- working with the Estonian Government to learn more about digital innovation and seconded a Marine Scotland official to Estonia when it held the EU Presidency in 2017;
- engaging with Norway on person centred care;
- learning from Finland's work on Universal Basic Income.

The European Union is built on the pooling and sharing of resources and powers with states retaining sovereignty. This approach fits in with that European cooperation and areas of common interest with the Nordics and Baltics. While Scotland sits outside the EU it will require greater focus and effort on keeping these links as inevitably the rest of Europe moves on from the chaos and bad faith of the Brexit period leaving us further behind. Scotland could help re-build those links and ironically may be a helpful lobbying source for the UK Government as it seeks to influence the decision-making process of its neighbour. In that way independence and a stronger relationship between Scotland and the EU and High North could be useful to the whole of the UK.

Our neighbours in these islands will be key partners and allies in the future as will our other neighbours. Professor Malcolm Chalmers, who is personally committed to the Union, said that: 'An independent Scotland has role models in places such as Denmark, Norway and Ireland especially those that are surrounded by friends.' Although he reminded me that while these relationships are important to maintain:

> Scotland needs to define itself in terms of the rest of the UK and will be its number one priority in much the same way that Norway's priority in 1905 was its relationship with Sweden and Denmark.

The relationship with the UK will remain Scotland's most important bilateral relationship in the same way as it is for Dublin and even to an extent Oslo.

* * *

However, Brexit has changed the dynamics within the UK and in the way we interact with our partners. The UK has moved away from the European Union and Scotland cannot sustain that relationship through Dublin and Brussels alone. Even engaging with Paris and Berlin is important but the close relationship and influence of our neighbours will be a powerful tool if Scotland is to remain close to the EU long-term and act as a bridge to help facilitate better relationships between London and Brussels. That is recognised elsewhere and Mariot Leslie remarked that, 'the Nordics take a similar world view to Scotland' and that 'Sweden would see Scotland as reinforcing the Nordic influence in the EU'. This has been a common theme when discussing the issue with politicians from the Nordic states.

To be successful in that endeavour one must not leave this simply up to politicians. Businesses and the third sector will play a key role as will universities. Mariot Leslie also noted from her time as Ambassador in Oslo of the number of Norwegians who were studying at Scottish universities. A relationship with Estonia was even helped by football when members of the Tartan Army travelling to Tallinn in the 1990s were so taken with the place that a number decided to stay. They set up businesses including the Highlander Scottish pub in Tallinn. I popped in when I was in town with an EU delegation and got chatting with Scots at the bar much to the astonishment of other EU colleagues. On that visit I remember an official from the local Irish Embassy saying that the Scots even had a stronger local brand than the Irish did.

If the Scottish Government's next Scotland House venture is to be in Copenhagen it will be important to ensure that is a cross sector endeavour that reaches out across the Baltic Sea.

* * *

Defence and security are a large part of our relationships with the Baltic and Nordic states. This is a big part of Nordic and Baltic policy cooperation given their history and the threats each faces. Estonia, Latvia and Lithuania are still relatively young countries. They have done remarkably well in steering their new states towards the European mainstream and, in so doing, building economically successful and vibrant states that are democratic, progressive and adhere to the rule of law. This has brought tangible benefits to citizens after the communist era.

The Soviet period that cast a shadow over the entire area is not entirely diminished and security remains a significant concern. Vladimir Putin makes no secret that he would reverse the fall of the Soviet Union if he could describing it as the 'greatest geopolitical catastrophe'.[218] The Baltics have nervously eyed up the actions of Russia elsewhere in the former Soviet Union not least the annexation of Crimea, part of Ukraine, its actions in Georgia and propping up a dictator in Belarus next door to them. The Baltic states have led the response to the crackdown on democracy protestors in Belarus often putting out statements from all three foreign ministries and leading the EU's response.

They are not immune to the continued threat from Putin's Russia as was proved by a massive cyber attack on Estonia in 2007 that evidence suggests was 'orchestrated by the Kremlin'.[219] They have reason to be nervous, within living memory residents of the Baltic states suffered dreadfully in the Soviet Union with the mass deportations of hundreds of thousands of citizens and other human rights violations.

That commitment to defence and working with other similar democratic states is important. Scotland could also provide important cultural and historic links in building relationships with Russia and in the far north. Fundamentally no one should be naive about the Putin administration in the Kremlin and its world view as well as an appalling domestic record when it comes to the rights of its own citizens. There are restrictions on freedom of expression, violence and torture in custody and attacks on human rights defenders, journalists and opposition politicians with Amnesty International stating that the human rights record of Russia 'continued to deteriorate'.[220] The Baltics and Nordics rightly expect to see solidarity from their democratic neighbours and friends in the EU and rest of Europe. Some of the bravest activists I have ever met were Russians who stood up to the authorities including lawyers arguing for the Rule of Law, LGBT activists who still had the marks of beatings from police and the mothers of Russian soldiers who were targeted for seeking information about their sons lost in Putin's wars.

Scotland's geographic location is important to our partners, and we need to take such considerations seriously. Rasmus Helveg Petersen highlighted what he sees as our importance to NATO:

> Scotland is strategically located because of the Iceland gap and dominates the southern part. That is an important bargaining chip for Scotland. It makes you interesting and it would be a strategic challenge if Scotland wasn't in NATO.

Former British Ambassador to Norway and NATO, Mariot Leslie, said that the Norwegians would be 'very pleased to be sure that Scotland is in NATO and to be able to work with Scotland'.

The same goes for Iceland and John MacDonald who founded the Scottish Global Forum, that helped facilitate discussion and debate about Scotland's place in the world on the run up to the 2014 Referendum, told me: 'NATO needs Scotland more than Scotland needs NATO' given the Iceland gap. When John MacDonald met with officials in Reykjavík, he said that the Icelandic officials were taking our future seriously and had clearly done their homework on Scotland.

Before the 2014 Independence Referendum the President of Iceland, Olafur Grimsson, even gave what was described as a 'cautious welcome' to the prospect of independence. In December 2012 he told BBC Newsnight:

> If you take a long-term view of about 100 years or so, the history of northern Europe is that countries have become independent one after the other. Whether Scotland will follow that route is a decision for the Scots to take. But despite difficulties that we have all faced, the moral of the story of independence in the North Atlantic – from Norway, through Iceland and growing self-rule in the Faroes and Greenland – is of course that the nations have fared quite well. Independence is not a disaster, but can be the road towards prosperity and a good society.[221]

Thinking in the SNP has also firmed up in a pro-NATO position with Alex Salmond telling the Brookings Institution in April 2013 that:

> As things stand, all air and naval policing in Northern Europe is coordinated through NATO. It makes sense, therefore, for Scotland to work within NATO on such important issues.

This is an area that our partners will be following closely and will have an impact on how Scotland is perceived. Finding common ground on defence does not simply mean acting as a counterweight to Russia. The Nordic states are reliable international partners in seeking and maintaining peace-building around the world including working with neighbours in every part of the former Soviet Union.

Along with Ireland, Norway won its seat on the UN Security Council in 2020 beating Canada. Norway has a long history of work at the UN and other international agencies and has committed to devote more attention during its tenure to make sure the UN considers how climate change affects peace and security. Prime Minister Erna Solberg said at the time:

> The world needs more international cooperation to promote peace and security. We will make use of our seat on the Security Council to strengthen this work.[222]

One would like to think a Scottish Foreign Ministry would have similar ambitions.

During the Cold War, Norway saw its 'smallness' and 'vulnerability' as being central to its foreign policy. The country understood that it had limited global influence on its own and was also in a challenging position during the Cold War given its proximity to the Soviet Union. That meant supporting a rules-based international system and what was considered to be the importance of 'maintaining political consensus on foreign policy'. Norway has played a key role in peace-building, as have other Nordic states, and as a 'smaller' state has been able to act as a peace broker not least with the Oslo Accords.[223]

Diplomats from across the Nordic states have played an outsized role in international organisations ever since such as the first ever UN Secretary-General Norway's Trygve Lie, Dag Hammarskjöld of Sweden who held the same role and Nobel peace laureate Martti Ahtisaari of Finland.

* * *

A key foreign policy plank that these states, similar in size and out-look, to Scotland is the importance of the rules-based system and international organisations. That is incredibly important to them all. 'We are members of pretty much any organisation that will have us,' one Nordic politician told me. It is very much a vision that Scotland should embrace. If the country is to be serious about its place in the world that means recognising our limitations and where we fit in at a global level.

Senior EU official and Danish-Scot Martijn Quinn has worked with various EU Commissioners and Member States. He agrees that there are lessons to be had from the Nordics naturally picking out Denmark:

> There is a lot Scotland can learn from the Nordics. We often look to Ireland but don't forget Scandinavia. Denmark is a great example that has done well in the EU, prosperous and successful with a population of five million and dealing with a large neighbour.

They are particularly good at being able to discuss and debate their differences, something that often needs to be learned in Scotland. Every year thousands of Danes including senior politicians head to the island of Bornholm for the *Folkemødet* (People's meeting). I met the organisers at a democratisation event in Nepal where it was described as like a political music festival or as another Dane I spoke to explained, 'T in the Park for political junkies'.

Bornholm is a great success, not just for the island's tourist industry that gets a big boost just before the height of the holiday season but also allows for discussion and socialising between Danes of all political groupings and none. I wonder if we could do some-thing similar. One of Scotland's islands would be a good host venue to attract people from the rest of the world such as Islay given the potential meeting space and other internationally recognised attrac-tions distilled there. It would be an incredibly attractive venue for potential participants.

Democratic and respectful discussion and debate are important, and the rules-based system should be sacrosanct. One Nordic poli-tician in Brussels told me, 'we feel aghast by what is happening in the UK and leaving behind a rules-based organisation'. The remarks outlined by Brandon Lewis that the UK Government was perfectly prepared to break international law over Brexit will have added to that concern. Even if the UK does not break the law in the end there has already been significant reputational damage. That is damaging across Europe with former French Europe Minister Natalie Louiseau, tweeting on 8 September 2020: 'you do break it or you don't. You can't be half illegal as you can't be half pregnant.'

Our cousins across to the north and east, as well as Ireland in the west, are comfortable with how they see themselves in the world. It is an idea of independence within an increasingly inter-dependent world where we join organisations and interact according to commonly agreed rules. A foreign policy that embraces the idea of multilateralism and is content not to be considered a great power but can play a role in international organisations. It is everything that Boris Johnson's Brexit project is not.

On that idea of joining the Nordic Council Danish academic Bjarke Dryer was worth listening to when he wrote:

> I will not discount what a massive impact centuries of shared history with your British compatriots has had. Nor will I claim that the Scandinavian contribution to your Gaelic heritage, a thousand years ago, should mean more to you. While we see the connection pop up in our languages, and in shared recessive genes, by any metric you have had more in common with the British for a very long time.

The relationship with the other parts of the British Isles are strong and will remain so regardless of Scotland's future. Brexit is not the entire history nor does it have a monopoly on our interactions. However, nothing, not least relationships between peoples, stands still. Just as the Baltic states 30 years ago, and Finland and Ireland a century ago, have had to consider, Scotland must decide where it stands in the world and what is important at this crucial point in its history.

There is also a lesson in how we interact with each other in these islands. The Nordics are perfectly comfortable working together with partnership and respect. In terms of identity, people are comfortable with a European, Nordic/Scandinavian and national identities. The question of identity does not necessarily place a restriction on our governing political institutions. Former SNP MSP Andrew Wilson argued in 1999 and again ahead of the 2014 Referendum that:

> the idea that Britishness and feelings of British identity could, should and would survive independence and should be no barrier to voting for it. My judgement was that a host of people I knew (including my own family) retained an enduring sense of common cause with the rest of Britain, having shared so much in life, especially in wartime and its aftermath.

Independence does not mean that a person who feels British loses that identity any more than leaving the EU takes away the European identity that many of us still have.

Bonds of identity exist beyond political structures and are perfectly illustrated by our neighbours. Some of those Nordic entities are fully independent such as Sweden, some are not, such as Greenland. Some sit within the EU, such as Denmark, others do not, such as Norway and Finland is even in the Euro whereas the others are not.

I cannot help but wonder if that model could be one for any future interaction with say Ireland and Scotland sitting within the EU as independent Member States and England sitting outside with a high degree of autonomy for other constituent parts. There is already precedent for some parts of these islands, the Isle of Man and Channel Islands have maintained high degrees of autonomy outside the EU just as the Faroes have and Greenland has experience both inside and out.

Historically we have been incredibly close to our Nordic neighbours. As we move forwards there is plenty we can learn from and build with them just as we have in the past.

CHAPTER 6

Britain Divided: The uk's Foreign Policy Divergences

The principle of the unlimited sovereignty of Parliament
is a distinctively English principle which has no
counterpart in Scottish constitutional law.

Lord Cooper, MacCormick v Lord Advocate, 1953

SCOTLAND HAS HAD a unique and distinctive foreign policy footprint since earliest times. There has always been an element of finding common ground with friends and neighbours just like in other countries. The Reformation and the two unions brought Scotland and England together and that will always remain an important relationship. For the most part that bilateral relationship will remain close and, even if Scotland is independent, the rest of the UK will be a key ally. However, in recent years there has been a sense of drift and divergence between Westminster and Holyrood not least in international affairs including the question of the relationship with our other European partners.

Scotland's politicians have taken a different overall view on issues such as Iraq, international development, climate change and migration among others and that is reflected in public attitudes. In some ways the differences have always been there but Brexit has brought them to a head with Westminster, and in particular the governing Conservative Party, placing an importance on the supremacy of parliamentary sovereignty and the ability to act unilaterally above other considerations such as the economy and the UK's diplomatic status. That is not an outlook on foreign policy widely shared in Scotland.

Looking at the key question of sovereignty it is not surprising that these differences have emerged given the different concepts that exist in Scotland and England. In the MacCormick constitutional law case in 1953 the judge, Lord Cooper, said: 'The principle of the unlimited sovereignty of Parliament is a distinctively English principle which has no counterpart in Scottish constitutional law.'[224] The English parliamentary tradition of sovereignty has taken precedence in the UK. This is not a purely academic question. Leaving the EU and giving sovereignty precedence will have an impact on our daily lives such as the price of food, holiday insurance, educational opportunities and other issues that people care about.

It also goes to the heart of how we see ourselves in the world. Scotland has not historically shared the idea of unlimited parliamentary sovereignty nor has it had a place in law as illustrated by Lord Cooper. The pooling and sharing of sovereignty, in this case with other European partners, is much easier to uphold and better understood by Scottish parliamentarians. It is one of the reasons why Scottish politicians were able to argue for and 'sell' the idea of the European project.

The BBC broadcaster Ros Atkins set out the differences in perceptions in London and Brussels which led to the difficulties in EU talks that he explained were about 'profoundly different visions of how countries pursue their interests' in a BBC news broadcast as talks came to a close in December 2020. BBC Europe Editor Katya Adler described the differences as 'a clash of ideologies'.

The Brexit talks were never 'just about trade' and finance. For the EU it is critical to the entire project to protect the Single Market as part of the wider peace project to bring Europe closer together. Even though this is the single biggest market on earth and on the UK's doorstep, the pro-Brexit ideologues in government do not want to be tied to the EU rules in any way. Sovereignty is therefore to be protected at all costs, and it will be costly. So uniquely in trade talks it was a negotiation over creating new barriers as the UK sought a mechanism of divergence from the rest of Europe. As Ros Atkins continues, the talks were about trying to square 'two very different ideas of how to organise our world'.[225]

Just as this goes some way to explaining the differences between the EU Member States and London's approaches it also goes some way to explaining the differences between Edinburgh and London. Scotland is much closer in world view to that in the remaining

27 EU Member States. It is why Brexit is so schismatic in the UK providing a very different backdrop and choice of futures for voters at a future independence referendum. At its core I believe this will be decided on how we see ourselves in the world in a way that wasn't the case in 2014.

International affairs is at the heart of the debate about Scotland's future more prominently than before though not of course for the first time. During the 1967 Hamilton by-election SNP candidate Winnie Ewing successfully campaigned on the slogan 'Stop the world Scotland wants to get on'. She has remained ever since a strong advocate of Scottish internationalism. When the Scottish Parliament was in the process of being established there were discussions over its international role by those on different sides of the constitutional debate such as Jack McConnell and George Reid.

That distinctive international policy and global footprint increased after 2007 with the election of the SNP in government. This was the first time that the party in power in Holyrood was different from that in Westminster. Although there had been some divergence between Westminster and Holyrood over the first eight years of devolution there were now two different parties with a very distinctive views of Scotland, and the UK's, places in the world.

Not since the Treaty of Union have those differences been as stark or as exposed as they are now. There has been talk of a 'clash of nationalisms' with an English nationalism led by Boris Johnson seeking a more unilateralist future that with fewer links with our neighbours and one in Scotland that sees the European Union and closer links across the continent as the future. The EU is of course set up to bring states closer together while leaving sovereignty in the Member States. Most Scots would prefer to see England inside the EU as a key partner. That will not be possible in the short-term but independence could be the jolt that returns our closest neighbours to the European fold.

* * *

The Brexit campaign and the establishment of the Scottish Parliament were not the only factors in driving divergence between Westminster and Holyrood in international affairs in recent years.

Popular opposition to the war in Iraq and the consequent chaos in that country was important. The conflict has had important consequences for politics across the UK and although the biggest driver of international affairs is domestic politics international events can drive political developments at home. I have lost count of the number of people I have spoken to who moved away from Labour in Scotland, often towards the SNP and independence because of Iraq. Actor Brian Cox told me that was a part of his journey from Labour to the SNP for example.

Iraq was a factor in the decline in support for Labour and Westminster more generally among Scottish voters, horrified by the scenes emerging from that country in the aftermath of the invasion. Crucially it has also forced NGOs in London, representatives of the international community and others to re-think the UK's role in the world. These have had an impact on the UK's willingness to act globally as witnessed in the debate over Syria with diminished confidence among parliamentarians and the public alike in the UK's institutions and foreign policy objectives.

The failures of the Iraq War are reasonably well-documented especially with the Chilcott Inquiry Report. The USA, UK and other coalition partners were able to rely on massive and overwhelming military superiority that meant that the war itself could be won in the short-term. Longer-term, the failure to secure the peace and the absence of effective post-conflict planning had a devastating impact on Iraq, costing the lives of hundreds of thousands and destabilising the entire region. Former British Ambassador to the UN, Jeremy Greenstock, told the Chilcott Inquiry: 'The preparations for the post-conflict stage were abject; wrong analysis, wrong people.'[226] This has since caused an erosion in trust for politicians in the UK and USA.

The Iraq War, and its well-documented failures, made the mistakes of intervention in Libya in 2011 even more difficult to understand. A foreign affairs inquiry into the intervention in Libya found that: 'UK Strategy was founded on erroneous assumption and an incomplete understanding of the evidence... the lessons of Iraq have not been learned.'[227] In Libya there was a problem, once again, with post-conflict planning and the committee report found that 'planners failed to appreciate that stabilisation and political reconstruction were preconditions for the successful implementation of normalisation plans'.

In research that I requested from the House of Commons when I was first elected in 2015, later included as evidence in the committee report, it was found that £320 million had been spent on the military campaign in Libya and just £25 million on reconstruction afterwards. That was a ratio of £1 being spent on peace-building for every £13 spent on the war. Surely the figures should have been the other way around to ensure long-term stability.

Action in Iraq and Libya have had an impact on how decision makers view military action. A few months after being elected I found myself on the Foreign Affairs Committee working with colleagues on an inquiry over whether the UK should be involved in air strikes against Daesh in Syria.[228] The debate within the committee was focused on the post-conflict planning and there was much discussion about a long-term solution. In the press release that accompanied the release of the report, the Conservative Committee Chair Crispin Blunt remarked:

> 'Just as we need a coordinated military strategy to defeat ISIL, we urgently need a complementary political strategy to end the civil war in Syria.'

Memories of the failures in Libya and Iraq were fresh in MPs' minds when it came to the vote on action in Syria. Two years before the case for military action in Syria was defeated in the House of Commons after a chemical weapons attack by Assad regime forces on civilians in August 2013 with then Labour leader Ed Miliband directly referencing the lessons of Iraq during the parliamentary debate.[229]

One of the key lessons from all of these events is that there must be more work on planning for post-conflict reconstruction. It was interesting to witness the thoughtful nature that many of the Foreign Affairs Committee members took to that long-term approach. There were concerns about the lack of capacity and the UK's ability to achieve its foreign policy objectives by MPs much more experienced than me, a number of whom had served in the armed services and had experienced war themselves.

It is difficult to avoid the conclusion that the UK has somewhat lost its way on foreign policy in recent years. As one former Foreign Office official told me the 'decline started with Iraq'. In his statement to Parliament on the day he resigned from Cabinet over the Iraq War Robin Cook told the Commons:

> Britain is not a superpower, our interests are best protected not by unilateral action but by multilateral agreement and a world order governed by rules.[230]

His resignation was triggered by what he saw as the diplomatic miscalculation of the Iraq invasion and the failure to gather international support for the conflict. His warnings of diplomatic isolation could equally be applied today.

The UK's decision to leave the EU is seen as another massive foreign policy failure with former House of Commons Speaker John Bercow describing it as 'the most colossal foreign policy blunder by the UK in the post-war period'.[231] Former Labour Europe Minister Denis MacShane wrote: 'Brexit is the biggest influence-reducing move ever seen in Britain's history of international relations.'[232]

Across the world there is presently a dimmer view of the UK amongst friends and allies than there has been for years. That is especially the case with Boris Johnson's leadership and the failures of UK politics and diplomacy that have led to Brexit chaos. Commentators elsewhere in the world have referred to a 'banana republic', 'stupid' and 'in decline' and allies looking on in horror at what has happened in what was once considered a reliable international partner.[233]

It is little wonder that the UK wants to recast itself with the government coming up with the idea of a post-Brexit 'Global Britain'. The main difficulty with that policy is that no one seems to know what it is or means. In another Foreign Affairs Committee Inquiry, we looked specifically at 'Global Britain' taking evidence from a range of foreign policy experts, senior officials and Ministers including then Foreign Secretary Boris Johnson. Everyone had a different understanding of the concept and the Report (agreed on a cross-party basis) reflected that 'none of the witnesses, however, could state clearly what the Global Britain policy entailed in practice'.[234]

* * *

As we looked at Scotland's relationship with the rest of Europe in the aftermath of Brexit there is an opportunity to look at how it fits into a multi-lateral world.[235] Many of those I have spoken to for this book have reflected on Scotland's place in the world and believe that its foreign policy must be grounded in multilateralism.

This is not new or even entirely Brexit related. In November 2013 the Scottish Government published its White Paper on independence which set out the multilateralist role that it envisaged for Scotland:

> Countries of a similar size to Scotland take lead roles in international organisations. Sweden, New Zealand, Switzerland and Finland have all made significant global contributions to security, peace and reconciliation initiatives: New Zealand, for example, played a key role in the Oslo Process that banned cluster bombs and similar weapons. These nations capitalise on their soft power and build coalitions – normally informal and related to specific issues – to advance their objectives.[236]

That aspiration is still relevant. It underlines the kind of Scotland that will emerge in the event of independence. One that is committed to multilateralism and working with other countries. It relies on an understanding that the country is not a global power backed up by military might but rather one that works with other countries and respects the international rules-based system. That stands in contrast to the UK which is committed to investing a further £200 billion in the latest generation of nuclear armament as a means of maintaining its global position.

Scotland will not be a nuclear power or a permanent member of the UN Security Council. It will have to do its international affairs in a different way relying on building agreement, the pooling of sovereignty and sharing resources. Scotland would therefore be much more aligned to its neighbours in the west such as Denmark and Norway.

That is backed up by conversations I have had with decision makers. Rasmus Helveg Petersen told me the basis for Denmark's foreign policy: 'We are members of everything, the UN, EU, NATO, OECD, Arctic Circle, Nordic Council, you name it'.

He talked about the importance of getting the big and small countries to abide by the rules and that gives everyone some protection. This is another area where Brexit has damaged how the UK is viewed in the world due to leaving the EU and its actions since such as the

UK's threat to break international law and as the only country in the world refusing to give its EU Ambassador diplomatic recognition.

The Danish MP's strong advice for Scotland was that:

> Scotland will have much more influence by harnessing multilateralism... England felt uncomfortable with being harnessed in that multi-lateral organisation. Brexit is a tragedy.

Rasmus was clear that he made his remarks as a friend of the UK who took no view on Scotland's constitutional future. These comments, like those of others, were said in a spirit of sadness about the UK rather than containing any animosity.

A similar world view is held in Norway who, like Denmark, has played a role in the world as a similar sized country to Scotland. Mariot Leslie the UK's former Ambassador to the country told me that they would be 'very pleased to be sure that Scotland is in NATO and to be able to work with Scotland'.

Ireland has similarly embraced multilateralism, although not a member of NATO and even back in the 1960s President Kennedy said of the country: 'This has never been a rich or powerful country, and yet, since earliest times, its influence on the world has been rich and powerful.'[237]

With independence Scotland would not have the same resources as the UK and would have to make choices based on its strengths and interests just as other countries do. These could be focused on the EU, climate justice and marine resources for example. It needn't necessarily wait for independence and these are areas that can be pursued without those normal powers and resource and recognition that comes with statehood.

One such area, where Scotland is increasingly seen as having a role to play, is that of peace-building and conflict resolution. Back in December 2003 I was involved in an initiative that brought the speakers of the parliaments of Georgia, Armenia and Azerbaijan to Craigellachie in Moray where they were hosted by the local MP Angus Robertson. It was the first time that the speakers of these South Caucasus parliaments had met and particularly significant that the Azerbaijanis and Armenians were willing to sit together. The initiative was driven by Dennis Sammut a former Maltese politician who runs the NGO Caucasus Links and had long seen Scotland's promise in this field. Angus Robertson said at the time:

> Craigellachie may seem like a strange place to hold peace
> talks, but the politicians will feel at ease here and can relax
> and talk about things they avoid at home.[238]

That ability to feel at ease was important for those involved in such tricky talks and it helped that Scotland was perceived to be, by participants, a safe space. The Moray countryside provided a relaxed venue where politicians could meet and talk openly with one another away from the challenges of day-to-day politics. The excellent whisky bar at the Craigellachie Hotel and an event hosted by the nearby Glenfiddich distillery also helped.

As well as acting as a safe space Scotland's peaceful constitutional journey was also an attraction. George Reid, then Presiding Officer, who had himself worked in the region hailed the South Caucasus Parliamentary Initiative as a 'great honour' for a Scotland whose devolved institutions were still new:

> To be here in Scotland together, to learn about how our
> parliament was established and to hear about our founding
> principles represents a significant commitment on their part
> to progressing their own institutions.

It helped that participants from the Caucasus and elsewhere in the former Soviet Union identify with and have a positive view of Scotland. No matter where I went in even the most remote parts of the former Soviet Union people had an awareness and understanding of Scotland. In South Ossetia I discussed Scotland's constitutional journey with local leaders and Scottish whisky with senior Russian officers stationed there.

The former MSP Andrew Wilson used a translation of Robert Burns in the local language, Ossetian, to build bridges during a visit. He even managed to use the Declaration of Arbroath which claims the Scots ended up in what is now Scotland having travelled from 'Greater Scythia' that could be claimed to include the South Caucasus. Using ancient myths to build connections is as old as diplomacy itself.

It was also helpful to use my own Scottish identity in some of the breakaway entity be it in South Ossetia, Nagorno-Karabakh or Abkhazia. Regardless of their views on Scotland's constitutional future most Scots I know who have worked in the region talk of their nationality as being a help. As one senior NGO official who works on some of the most intractable conflicts told me being Scottish is an 'easy-opener' no matter who you are speaking to.

* * *

Scotland's opportunity in peace-building goes beyond the South Caucasus. Mark Muller Stuart has worked in areas affected by conflict throughout the world as a Senior UN Mediation Adviser. He has talked regularly about Scotland's potential in peace-building. In his book *Storm in the Desert* Mark writes about his experiences of the conflict in Libya and reflections on politics and diplomacy. In the book he comments that when he was watching the debate on the Iraq War in 2003, he found the idea of Scotland having its own distinct foreign policy 'counter-intuitive' but has now changed his mind and writes:

> I have been constantly struck by how emerging leaders from around the world enjoy and are ready to embrace Scotland as a small but vibrant, soft power nation with an extraordinary historical brand and important constitutional story to tell.
>
> My experiences as an international human rights advocate and mediator convince me Scotland has a real and unique contribution to make in the field of conflict resolution, and in the promoting of mutual understanding between nations and cultures.

When we meet at his home at Traquair House in the Borders, he builds on these observations in his book and tells me:

> In terms of Scotland's foreign policy, it [Scotland] doesn't need to be independent for a lot of roles such as peace-building, the rule of law and poverty alleviation. You can't do all this within the Union but if you do that Union has to be renewed significantly to properly take on board Scotland and its role.

The arc of history points in favour of a greater Scottish voice in international affairs and those who want to restrict that won't be successful.

The festivals, NGOs like Beyond Borders etc. show you Scotland has a big imprint and global conscience, so it has an ability to pursue soft power diplomacy. People will take Norwegian money and talk to those stakeholders, but most would rather do that in Scotland.

Scotland has an ability to become a place for global diplomacy but only if it can express its own identity in a new Union or independence but not in the current system especially with Brexit.

Mark has put his belief in Scotland's potential to the test in his work and founded Beyond Borders Scotland. The organisation is based in Edinburgh and the Scottish Borders bringing people together for dialogue and cultural exchange. Its website describes its work as:

> dedicated to facilitating international dialogue and cultural exchange between nations. The organisation aims to create a vibrant international platform within Scotland, to break down borders between peoples, and help facilitate wider international cultural exchange, dialogue and reconciliation.[239]

It draws participants from the business, diplomatic, media and academic communities as well as across the political spectrum in Scotland. As Mark tells me Beyond Borders has been able to build what he calls a 'small peace-building role because Scotland can play a plucky role given its brand'. Positioning itself in Scotland is important to the work but crucially Mark's vision, leadership and impressive contacts book has also played a major role in demonstrating Scotland's potential through Beyond Borders' work.

Every year Beyond Borders brings together people from across the world for discussion and debate at the Beyond Borders International Festival. These have included the 'Art of Peace-building', 'Democracy in the Digital Age', 'Pakistan on the Brink' and the war in Syria.

These are just a few examples of the rich and diverse range of events bringing in some of the most interesting speakers and artists that you will find at any festival.

Mark is not alone in seeing Scotland's potential. There is scope for Scotland to engage and build on its peace-building work inside or outside the Union. Former First Minister Jack McConnell told me that Scotland could play a key role in peace-building and conflict resolution especially after the experience of peaceful constitutional change in 1999: 'Most conflicts in the world today are about majorities and minorities and can only be resolved with a political solution for the minority.'

Jack McConnell has taken that message to the Philippines among other places using his experiences of devolution to help build autonomous sub-state governments as well as advising the central authorities on the value that devolution can bring.

The former Labour First Minister has a point about Scotland's experiences and people have spoken to me about our peaceful constitutional journey, that no one should ever take for granted. Sabir Zazai of the Refugee Council who fled Afghanistan and was himself affected by conflict says: 'Scotland has a role to play in helping others seek justice without reaching for guns,' and continues, 'how did we get to the point that devolution is respected?' Sabir Zazia also told me that there are lessons to be learned across the world where those involved in conflict 'can relate to the Westminster and Holyrood context' where we debate powerful differences in a peaceful fashion.

Dealing with the refugee crisis can be important in how you see and are seen in the world. During the summer of 2020 there was a huge amount of concern among politicians and the media around the 'migrants' crossing the channel to Kent. In one television clip a group in a boat were asked where they came from, 'Iraq' came the reply. This is the Iraq that had been invaded by the UK, who had failed to plan for the aftermath of that conflict resulting in a devastating civil war. They were refugees from Iraq and instability that had been caused, in part, by the country where they now sought refuge.

How we deal with the vulnerable is an important message to the world and it is worth considering why people become refugees. It is not through choice but through desperation. Meeting refugees is a powerful experience that reminds you of the plight that they face and why an act of welcome means so much. I remember when I saw the work of the wonderful Dundee-based charity For the Love of a Child near the Syrian border in Lebanon. Donna Jennings was helping support a safe space for small children. The lady running the centre was herself a refugee who had fled her home in such dangerous circumstances that as she fled with her children she carried nothing except her youngest son who was two. By the time she reached safety the boy had gone limp having been shot by a stray bullet as the family fled and died in her arms. Heart-breaking as it was, her story was not unusual.

Making 'Refugees Welcome' is a powerful message to those who have experienced such horrors and one that Scots should be proud of. It also shows the long-term nature of stabilisation efforts and that your overseas policy has an impact at home. Like the lady I met in Lebanon and so many others refugees leave their homes in the most desperate circumstances. As the cross-party Foreign Affairs Committee noted in the report on the UK's intervention in Libya:

> the UK has a particular responsibility in relation to migrants
> and refugees, an issue which has been exacerbated by the
> collapse of the Libyan state.[240]

Foreign policy may be driven by domestic politics, but it can never be short-term. The aftermath of the conflicts in Libya, Iraq, Afghanistan and elsewhere requires long-term planning. The rebuilding efforts after conflict take decades, even now a quarter-century after the peace accords in Bosnia-Hercegovina the country is still in need of international assistance and attention in those rebuilding efforts.

As part of our inquiry into Libya, the Foreign Affairs Committee visited Tunis, where the Foreign Office's staff working in that country were based because of security. We met the UK's Ambassador to Libya, Peter Millet, who was doing fantastic and brave work along with other officials. Unfortunately, the security situation did not allow for a visit to the Libya, but we met with several people from the country. The Ambassador was working with youth groups and we saw a news programme that was produced by young Libyans for young Libyans backed by the British Council. Fantastic work being done by far sighted officials and at a fraction of the cost of military intervention.

Libya was failed, in part, because of the lack of post-conflict planning as well as the short attention span of some politicians. One UN worker who had spent time in Libya during and after the intervention told me that for half the price of a cruise missile they could have funded a project to stabilise civil society in Benghazi in eastern Libya but although the cash was forthcoming for the conflict it was not for stabilisation. Further military action was still being considered when we visited in 2016 and we were briefed by officials on relatively advanced plans for a military expedition of several thousand troops from Spain, the UK and elsewhere in Europe to land in Tripoli. The plan was abandoned shortly after our visit but caused concern among the MPs.

Investing, long-term in stabilisation and soft power is critical for long-term foreign policy objectives. In the run up to the Iraq War it has been reported that former Secretary of State Colin Powel referred to the 'Pottery Barn' rule of international affairs, 'You break it, you own it'. That means you cannot simply take military action and walk away, countries need to invest and plan for the long-term consequences of their actions.[241] Even when there is not direct involvement long-term reconstruction efforts take decades, as will be the case in Syria once the war, that has devastated the country, comes to an end.

Scotland could focus its work on the post-conflict reconstruction efforts rather than just military action itself. Experience tells us that more efforts and resources will need to go into rebuilding than any military 'victory'.

There are valuable lessons around devolution that others may benefit from. Simon O'Connell the former Executive Director of Mercy Corps Europe, who now heads up the Dutch international development organisation SNV (Netherlands Development Organisation/ *Stichting Nederlandse Vrijwilligers*), talks about other countries learning from Scotland's experiences of decentralisation and fighting poverty through 'better, fairer, more localised and inclusive systems of governance'. In a speech to the Royal Scottish Academy in November 2017 Mark Muller Stuart told the audience:

> Scotland has a phenomenal story to tell. Its devolved settlement is in fact one of the best examples of how smaller nations within larger states can transition towards greater democracy in a peaceful and consensual manner.[242]

Several countries were highlighted by different practitioners I spoke to who could benefit from discussing Scotland's story. These have included Nepal, Democratic Republic of Congo and Lebanon as well as across the former Soviet Union and beyond. Groups have also visited Scotland to learn more about its story including those from Turkey, Kurdistan, Georgia, Ukraine, Syria, Oman, India and Sri Lanka to name just a few.

In Colombia I met with those involved in the peace process who knew about Scotland's constitutional journey and were interested. In Erbil, Iraq, Turkey, Bahrain and elsewhere where there is a need for decentralisation, better representation and a greater dialogue. People are aware of Scotland, its story and there is further potential. Mark Muller Stuart has even discussed Scotland with Kurdish leader Abdullah Ocalan in his prison in Turkey.

There has also been interest and work on the conflict in Syria from the highest levels of the UN. In May 2016 the UN Special Envoy to Syria, Staffan de Mistura, brought ten members of the UN Women's Advisory Board to Scotland. The board had been established under Security Council Resolution 1325 that recognises the role of women in the resolution and prevention of conflict. The focus of the talks was on the conflict in Syria with the Scottish Government providing some finance and Scotland providing a safe space, as Staffan de Mistura observed:

> The very special case of Scotland – currently with its own parliament and strong gender balance in government and the fact that the First Minister and two opposition leaders [Ruth Davidson and Kezia Dugdale] are women – were key motivating factors in helping set this up… What I do realise is that even when you are not independent you do still have a very specific message to give that has international resonance.'[243]

Beyond Borders and Mark were central to bringing this group to Scotland and facilitating the visit. Groups have since brought together women peace-makers from Iraq, Libya, Yemen and Syria to Scotland. This was hopefully helpful for the UN in their work, provided a safe space for those affected by conflict and gave Scottish policy-makers first-hand experience of engaging with those impacted by conflict and witnessing the UN at work. Jessica Forsythe, the Deputy Director of Beyond Borders Scotland said:

> Beyond Borders is pleased to support this important initiative, bringing the Syrian Women's Advisory Board to Scotland. Scotland has an impressive record of female leaders in politics as well as a unique non-violent constitutional journey.[244]

Nicola Sturgeon spoke of this work at the United Nations in July 2017, a project she hoped 'will play a part in establishing peace, rather than simply coping with the consequences of war'.[245] I also raised this work and Scotland's role at a meeting with the UN Secretary-General, Antonió Guterres, the following year on a Foreign Affairs Committee visit.

This is a view shared by many working in the sector. Jonathan Cohen who heads up Conciliation Resources a London-based NGO working on conflict throughout the world talks up the 'soft power' role that Scotland can play. He highlights that Scotland has been a 'good faith actor' and that Scotland could have a 'distinctive multi-lateral agenda'.

Tom Meredith, former Chief Executive at the John Smith Trust who now works at the HALO Trust, based in Dumfriesshire, that helps communities recovering from conflict. He talked of the opportunities for Scotland as he says the 'Scottish identity isn't as loaded' and that could be important 'when dealing with difficult terrain such as the relationship with Russia'. Tom and others talk of the good work undertaken by Scottish organisations here and such as the work HALO had done 'engaging with Police Scotland on violence reduction'.

Former senior British Foreign Office official Craig Oliphant has also found that Scotland could have a distinctive role to play. 'There are no two ways about it – Scotland has much to offer in the soft power realm' and 'a lot of scope to engage externally'. Craig talks about Scotland's distinctive opportunity that it has to complement UK foreign policy and that 'outside the independence debate it makes sense for Scotland to up its game and play to its strengths'.

His experience even tells him that Scotland could be a better option for some groups rather than pursuing the more familiar schedule of visiting Northern Ireland. Some may prefer to think that they don't have the same problems as in the Northern Ireland context and are 'not sure they are comfortable with possible parallels drawn for their own protracted situation with Northern Ireland'.

A good example would be the experience of police reform in Scotland which provides accessible and important practical insights. That is not to deny the undoubted valuable lessons to be gained by many groups provided from Northern Ireland. And, ultimately, it is not a case of 'either, or' but rather the model that best suits the visitors. It is rather to say that both have distinctive offers for peacebuilders to choose from and visits to both can be complementary as a learning experience.

Craig Oliphant highlighted a visit to Dundee with a group of Armenians who were impressed by their engagement with David Hamilton at Police Scotland and the Council leader John Alexander. He said that the group

> got considerable value from their day-long visit to Dundee, and to such an extent that it represented the highlight of their visit for the granular experience and good practice shared.

> It's the accessible nature of Scotland with its institutions, engagement with young people (YoungScot, YouthLinkScotland, Scottish Youth Parliament) and organisations like Police Scotland, COSLA and others who are so willing to engage... You could always guarantee a genuine and frank engagement in Scotland. In diplomatic terms that is huge.

Combining a Scottish element of their programme of work with that in London brings two different but complementary perspectives. That is a lesson that the John Smith Trust has been aware of for years. Their fellowships have a distinctive element of their visit in London, but they always spend time in Scotland as well. It is clear from meeting the Fellows the deep attachment they maintain for Scotland afterwards and the importance of that experience.

The work done over decades by the trust's founder Baroness Smith and her family has been pivotal to the success of the trust. The networks that the trust have built up provide a fantastic resource helping those from areas affected by conflict to reach out if they wish where dialogue can otherwise be difficult. It has also proved an invaluable resource for British embassies who are able to draw on a community of local leaders and influencers with a positive memory of the UK and Scotland.

* * *

From conversations with those who have been affected by conflict and those working in this area it is clear that Scotland's distinctive brand and story is incredibly important. There is plenty of potential for more work in this area by the Scottish Government and the Foreign Office for that matter. Mark Muller Stuart said in his book on Libya:

> I have been constantly struck by how emerging leaders from around the world enjoy and are ready to embrace Scotland as a small but vibrant, soft power nation with an extraordinary historical brand and important constitutional story to tell... Whether Scotland becomes independent or remains within an enduring political union in the UK as a consequence of the Brexit vote of 23 June 2016, the time has surely come to ask how Scotland can play a greater role in international affairs.[246]

The Scottish brand is important to our businesses but it is also important to the peace-building community. In his speech to the Royal Scottish Academy Mark also talked about the country having a 'strong separate identity, which exercises a powerful hold over the world's collective imagination.'[247]

Tom Meredith observed that rightly or wrongly 'we don't have the perceived agenda of HMG [Her Majesty's (UK) Government] overseas.' Tom talked about some of the feedback that he had received from John Smith Fellows, all influential one way or another in their own societies, that their impressions of Scotland had been 'accessible', 'an easy place to integrate', 'transparency', 'accessibility of Ministers, industry and the media'. That gives you a very good start for further work.

Jonathan Cohen talked about the impact of our sporting and cultural achievements. Sport (and any sporting 'achievements') might sound like a strange place to start but it gives you recognition. Jonathan reminisced that he had learned about geography by following his team Liverpool. My own experiences are as a Dundee United supporter when people know who you are from European competitions, and you have that common language of football.

Culturally the Edinburgh festivals bring people together from around the world and were started to help rebuild relationships after the Second World War and still bring people together to this day. Those festivals were also highlighted as an area where Scotland has a positive story to tell.

Education is another sector that has a role to play in Scotland's branding and internationalisation. Former Labour Cabinet Minister Douglas Alexander described the higher education sector as a 'sleeping giant' in Scotland. It can help with reach and building influence, many who have studied in Scotland, even for a short time, leave with a positive view. Working in Brussels I recall Scottish industry would often get a hearing from a senior German member of the Industry Committee who had studied at the University of Edinburgh and had a self-confessed soft spot for the country. Others struggled to get that kind of access to MEPs from other Member States and plenty of others have similar stories to tell from Brussels and elsewhere.

Interviewees commented on Scotland's leadership in areas such as medical research, renewables and the legacy of the Enlightenment. In a speech to the Scottish Parliament in June 2001, then President Mbeki of South Africa talked at length of the impact of Scotland in his country and especially education:

> Perhaps as important, it was in the area of education that the Scottish influence was felt most... For over more than a century, Scottish educational institutions admitted many South Africans, especially black South Africans, who went on to become great leaders in South Africa.[248]

The President praised the cities of Glasgow and Aberdeen that made such a difference to the anti-apartheid struggle. Others have talked about the impact that Scotland's city regions could have in foreign policy. That positivity went beyond South Africa in that part of the world. I spent some time working with parliamentarians in Namibia where the Speaker of the Parliament Peter Katjavivi spoke of his fond memories of time in Glasgow during his exile in the UK. Peter was head of SWAPO's (South West African People's Organisation) overseas office in London and several SWAPO members who played an important role in the establishment of 'the Namibian' newspaper had been exiled to Glasgow.

Thabo Mbeki also spoke of the influence that Scotland could have in the future in helping Africa achieve its potential telling Holyrood:

> Our great hope is that the 21st century will be the African century. We are certain that the Scottish people and the Scottish Parliament will help us realise this historic objective.

The case of Africa and its relationship with Scotland is worth further exploration. Scots were at the heart of the British Empire and we must own and be honest about our past. There can be no place for mythmaking, and we must embrace the good with the bad. Sabir Zazai touched upon Scotland's history during our conversation:

> These are not all happy elements, but we can learn from them all... Scotland has many examples of how we have contributed globally. Sad history still contributes.

Some have said that Scotland must look beyond its relationship with Malawi in its approach to international affairs. I have some sympathy with extending relationships as well as Malawi, but it is a long-lasting relationship where key work has been done and a very worthwhile partnership with some important lessons overall not least the work done by David Hope-Jones and his colleagues at the Scotland Malawi Partnership. In 2020 as the Black Lives Matter campaign resonated across the globe the Malawi-Scotland partnership who coordinate Malawi's links with Scotland and the Scotland Malawi partnership who do the same job in Scotland put out a joint statement. That statement began:

> We acknowledge and greatly regret that racism has been perpetrated in Scotland's 161-year relationship with Malawi, while also appreciating that there are a great many examples of Scots and Malawians working together to fight prejudice.

The document continued to reflect, in a balanced way, about the impact that some Scots had on the country and the support for the independence movement in the country. It did not sugar coat Scotland's role in the British Empire and the damage that was done especially the slave trade. The joint statement finishes:

> It is essential that we look to understand this history, to high-
> light the wrongs that have been done and learn from them
> and use the contemporary Scotland-Malawi relationship as
> a powerful force for good, driven by both nations.

In the face of history and grave injustices highlighted by the Black Lives Matter movement it is easy to feel helpless and overwhelmed by the vastness of this legacy. The joint statement is a good way of seeking to bring nations closer together by acknowledging mistakes of the past and building a forward-looking relationship.

We would not be alone in pursuing this work as other countries of a similar size do this. Back in 1963 President Kennedy praised Ireland's role in Kashmir. Across the Irish sea the Norwegians have developed a particularly strong peace-building role while remaining active members of NATO. There are areas worth exploring further. In evidence to the Scottish Parliament Anthony Salamone looked at why Norway had been successful:

> Norway's most visible international role is in conflict res-
> olution as an international peace-builder and mediator.
> A collection of factors, including those above, has enabled
> it to achieve a high global profile in this area. Norway is a
> relatively recent independent state (since 1905) and does not
> have the imperial past of many of its European neighbours.[249]

Norway has worked on difficult areas as a peace-builder across the world and Salamone highlights the country's work in 'Kosovo, Yugoslavia, Northern Ireland and Somalia to Colombia, Palestine and the Iran nuclear deal'. It has focused on what it does well in this area and is helped by not being a big power and having no such aspi-rations. Recognising your own limitations including those of size, capacity and history plays an important part in developing an effec-tive international policy.

* * *

Independence would bring benefits such as a Foreign Ministry, membership of the UN and international recognition. That would be my preference of course but even without independence an enhanced role for Scotland can be achieved within the Union. The international community is starting to recognise the role that we could play in peace-building and conflict resolution. As those working for NGOs have acknowledged there could be a role for Scotland given our political story in recent years and the fact that the Scottish Government has a distinctive policy agenda from the UK Government. That means a different relationship with international partners.

Beyond conflict the UK could make more of Scotland's brand and soft power in other areas too. Trade is one such area as former Brexit campaigner and Conservative MEP David Campbell Bannerman acknowledged where he said the diaspora could be a means of reaching into the USA especially the states. That is just one country where Scotland does have a strong recognised brand and a track record of positive engagement with elected representatives and millions who identify with our country.

On a visit to Washington DC in 2018 with the Foreign Affairs Committee we received a briefing from the British Ambassador about the latest trade negotiations. Ambassador Kim Darroch was getting a hard time, not least from Conservative members, about the country's perceived lack of clout in the White House and Congress. There was an admission that very few elected members were taking part in briefings on the UK's trade position and they were looking at ways to improve engagement. The day after that meeting I met with one of the Scottish Government officials based in at the British Embassy in Washington DC who told me that their events in Congress to promote Scottish produce had been busy with elected members from across the USA both Republican and Democrat.

It is easy to see why elected members took an interest when members of the Scots diaspora make up a big proportion of the electorate in all 50 states. Naturally politicians want to show support for and engagement with the 'old' country. The Scottish diaspora has political and economic clout. Despite this the UK Government had never made use of the Scottish Government's soft power even though it has significant political reach that could complement that of the UK.

The same failure was seen in another area where Scotland is seen to be leading that of climate change. We looked at the failure to engage with Scotland in Copenhagen in 2009. There is a concern that the UK Government could be about to make the same mistake at the next UN Climate Change Conference, COP26, in Glasgow that will draw global attention.

Climate change is the biggest challenge of this generation. It will continue to be an area where Scotland can build on its work and international outreach especially on the run up to those climate talks. Cooperation between the different administrations in the UK is not looking positive. Claire O'Neill, who served as a Conservative MP and Minister and the former COP26 Event Coordinator, said given Scotland's 'great track record' on the environment, that:

> I did suggest that we give Nicola Sturgeon a job and she was involved in this, which the Prime Minister heartily and saltily rebutted.[250]

That is a disappointing and short-sighted approach by the British Government. Across areas of foreign policy, the UK could and should be making more of Scotland's foreign policy footprint as part of a decentralised approach that takes advantages of the soft power strengths of its constituent parts. When I highlighted the work that had been done in the area of peace-building by NGOs and practitioners drawing on Scotland's brand and story in the House of Commons the Foreign Office Minister, Alan Duncan, responded: I must say that his notion of the soft power of Robbie Burns' poetry solving the conflicts in Georgia rather stretched me.[251]

The comments by Alan Duncan and Claire O'Neill, both thoughtful Ministers who felt ill at ease in a Johnson Government, does not bode well for those Ministers who remain. Indeed, there is significant concern that has been expressed by politicians, officials and others close to the UK Government around its ability and commitment to working with the Scottish Government as a true partner. One former Foreign Office official told me:

> If London can't recognise the strong assets it has in Scotland then does it not make sense for Scotland to get on with what it does well in terms of external relations.

Jonathan Cohen of Conciliation Resources also said: As Boris Johnson pursues the UK national interest could Scotland pursue a distinctive multilateralist agenda. Mark Muller Stuart also commented on this in his Royal Scottish Academy speech in November 2017 saying:

> Scotland has a profound contribution to make in the field of peace building, conflict resolution and wider cultural exchange between different nations, cultures and religions. The time has surely come for UK policy-makers to consider whether these islands should adopt a more innovative, asymmetrical, full-spectrum approach to conflict resolution, in which the power of state and non-state actors, hard and soft power institutions, as well as the nations in our Kingdom, work in partnership in the service of cultural diplomacy and peace-making.

Chris Deerin of Reform Scotland said that Brexit makes it possible for Scotland to be 'good cop to England's bad cop' in foreign policy.

That distinction and acceptance of multilateralism and pooling sovereignty that is accepted in Scotland but rejected by an 'isolationist' government in Whitehall provides space for Scotland to pursue its owns ideas. That is even possible, though more restricted, within the confines of the Union.

Professor Caron Gentry, Head of the School of International Relations at the University of St Andrews has argued that Scotland could lead the way in pursuing a Feminist Foreign Policy (FFP). She has told me that this is an area where that would particularly suit the leadership of Nicola Sturgeon. The First Minister has already been appointed by UN Women as the 'first global advocate for the UN's #HeForShe campaign'.[252] Nicola Sturgeon also told the UN in a speech in July 2017 that she wanted to see progress on gender issues both in Scotland and elsewhere:

> my country will take a lead in trying to drive forward progress – both within Scotland, but also, where possible, by helping promote gender equality beyond our own borders... we were the first country in the world to establish a climate justice fund – helped to empower women.[253]

In an article for Reform Scotland published in August 2020 Professor Gentry looks at FFP and how Scotland could lead in this area. It begins by setting out what constitutes an FFP:

> FFP does not just addresses women's material positions around the world but embraces a 'reorientation' of foreign policy based upon cosmopolitan ideals of justice, peace, and pragmatic security. A feminist foreign policy listens to marginalised voices and aims to remove gender, racial, sexual, and socio-economic boundaries, amongst others. It is empathetic, sensitive, caring, and relational.

It then sets out where Scotland fits into this description by both looking at the nation's domestic and foreign policy agenda:

> And this is where Scotland enters the picture. Contemporary Scottish politics are inherently feminist. They may not be known as such — perhaps the word feminism is too scary or off-putting. With devolution and the parties that have held the most power in Holyrood, Scottish voters have noted their interest in politics and policies that emphasise equality of all kinds, parity, justice and fairness. Scottish policies aim to create a society that removes barriers rather than foster them. Policies like these will, eventually, inherently upend masculinist power structures. The combined strength of the SNP, Labour, Greens, and Liberal Democrats in Scotland demonstrates a population interested in social, economic, and climate justice. As a nation moves its political agenda beyond its borders it does so only based upon the issues and politics that are cared about internally. The Scottish vote to remain in the EU demonstrates the population's desire to be part of cosmopolitan inter-governmental organisations.

Professor Gentry told me that Scotland is already 'following an unrealised Feminist Foreign Policy' given some of the priorities pursued by the SNP and other political parties that she says shows a commitment to 'people not institutions'. She cites her experiences of arriving in Scotland and as an American being impressed when she found out there was no charge for prescriptions. She added the observation that Scotland is already pursuing a foreign policy that is more 'multilateralist' and closer to the Nordics than some aspects of UK foreign policy.

It is interesting that Professor Gentry and others make direct reference to Scottish domestic policy as the main driver of foreign policy. Holyrood gives us the framework for identifying what our foreign policy looks like and where it may expand if Scotland has its own Ministry of Foreign Affairs with the reach and resource that would bring.

* * *

An honest, non-partisan and open appraisal about Scotland's role within or independent of the UK is important. Far too often in today's discourse one sees a huge amount of polarisation. Holding a different political view is seen as a characteristic flaw rather than an honestly held opinion. The extremes are active on social media with abuse towards those they disagree with often hiding behind anonymous accounts. Women and minorities often bear the brunt of that abuse.

So, we must be honest and pluralistic in conducting our own debate if we are to have a mark on the world and be able to be an honest broker in some of the world's most complicated conflicts. There is an opportunity as the UK steps back from multilateralism and there is uncertainty about what 'Global Britain' means.

That recognition is a positive development but one that will bring its own challenges. How we debate Scotland's constitutional future and treat one another will have an impact on our soft power potential. The debate around Brexit has diminished the UK's soft power just as surely as the actual act of leaving the EU damaged its brand.

Mark Muller Stuart observed in his book on Libya in the section entitled 'Scotland's Emerging Role in International Affairs' that:

> it ill behoves any policy-maker serious about improving the peace-making record of the UK not to recognise Scotland's growing capacity to act in this area. The positive values that underpin Scotland's civic nationalism and humanitarianism can only make it a greater force for good in the world.

That also means being realistic and having a mature debate over global affairs. We shouldn't excuse say the violence of Spanish police towards voters and the imprisonment of Catalan politicians any more than we should overlook Russia's appalling human rights record. We must be realistic in engaging with our partners and expect them to maintain international norms regardless of how that fits into our domestic politics.

That means standing up to Saudi Arabia over Yemen and difficult decisions over arms exports. The war in Yemen is one of the worst humanitarian crises in the world and we cannot afford to turn a blind eye.

Similarly, no one should forget the Kremlin's devastating wars and the regret of many in power there over the hard-won independence of its neighbours, many of them natural partners to Scotland. Let's not forget independence from the Soviet Union that has seen citizens' rights and standard of living improve in the Baltic states and elsewhere. We must also stand with Russia's citizens. Sitting with human rights advocates in Russia is a powerful antidote to much of the Kremlin propaganda in a country where being an activist, opposition politician or journalist is a dangerous business.

There must also be regard for democracy and due process. There was huge respect across the world for the way in which the previous Independence Referendum was carried out. That has resonance for countries who have been unable to have the same respectful non-violent debate around issues that generate such passion.

That is also important to our neighbours in Europe. In the book *Scotland's Referendum and the Media* Klaus Peter Müller observed in the section on how it was perceived in Germany, Austria and Switzerland that: 'Consumers of these media will have gained a favourable understanding of Scotland, wherever its impressive democratic process has been described.'[254]

Ensuring that there is due process and respect for each other and democracy will be critical to maintaining the branding that has been built up on these issues. As one NGO leader said to me 'procedure is everything'. That will provide a challenge for those in favour of independence who are increasingly frustrated by the lack of engagement by the UK as well as those in favour of the Union who cannot continue to deny repeated mandates and majorities for a referendum given the undeniable change in circumstances that Brexit brought.

People also need to be realistic about the choices that we face in the future. There is now a very distinctive choice between a UK outside the EU and an independent Scotland within it. There is clear red, white and blue water. Lazy assumptions over nationalism no longer apply with Brexit seen as an English nationalist project that turns its back on neighbours, stops freedom of movement of it UK citizens (alone among its neighbours) and is hostile to immigration. On the other hand, Irish politicians regularly describe themselves as 'nationalists' while pursuing an internationalist agenda. As Alex Salmond once told the Brookings Institution in Washington DC: 'self-determination cannot mean isolation, and nationalism must embrace internationalism'.[255]

CHAPTER 7

Building Scotland's International Future

*Small, peaceful countries can exercise major global
influence... based not on military power and alliances,
but on values and ideals.*[256]

Alex Salmond, Trinity College Dublin,
13 February 2008

EVERY COUNTRY TAKES a slightly different approach to conducting
its foreign policy. Those policies will reflect that country, its culture,
politics and how it sees itself in the world. Just as domestic politics is
the biggest driver of international politics so too is a state's internal
constitutional set-up a driver in how it conducts itself internationally. How we conduct our international affairs tells us a bit about the
country and how we see ourselves in the world. Scotland is an actor
in international affairs, hidden in plain sight. That role will evolve
and further develop over the next few years as Scotland decides what
kind of country it wants to be.

The UK's place in the world is undergoing a period of dramatic
change, there is no such thing as the status quo. Scotland must also
make its choices in how it fits into that new world. How we interact with each other tells our friends and partners about the kind
of country we aspire to be. During my time on the Foreign Affairs
Committee I was fortunate to be able to see the workings of different
states at close-up that told me a bit about them.

In Saudi Arabia it is very clear that foreign policy is driven
from the very top. In a meeting with Crown Prince Mohammad Bin
Salman of Saudi Arabia we spent time questioning him on his foreign
policy including the conflicts in which the country was, and still is,
involved. It was clear that he was fully in charge with the Foreign

Minister remaining quiet as his boss spoke. We watched aides stand by, ready to fill up his glass of tea or take away it away depending on a flick of the hand.

In Russia we met with our counterparts on the Committee for International Affairs at the State Duma. There was no disagreement between the Russian members even on the tough questions around Crimea, Ukraine or Syria in the same way that our committee reflected many different views. The shared opinion appeared to be that Vladimir Putin was doing an admirable job with no dissent that we heard. When I managed to speak to the Depute Chair alone on the way to the lift, she was most interested in how she could get a round at the Old Course in St Andrews.

In China we all sat in carefully pre-assigned seats depending on our 'seniority' with limited interaction with colleagues in Beijing. As part of a cross-party grouping led by then Deputy Prime Minister David Lidington we met with politicians in the Chinese capital and later in Wuhan. Meetings were carefully choreographed and although each parliamentarian was able to get in some words, and we raised issues like the rule of law, human rights and climate change, there was little scope for meaningful discussion.

There was much more common ground with those who shared a commitment to democracy and the rule of law. This was obviously the case with European partners who shared a similar world outlook and it was easy to find areas of agreement. Even in the USA during the Trump presidency there were enough people who believed in democracy and the rule of law – and that will certainly be the case with a Biden administration. There was an understanding of the need to build and maintain alliances with other like-minded states who were committed to democracy, human rights, free trade and the rule of law across the world but especially in Europe.

Scotland would very much fit in with those other like-minded states in the EU because of how we conduct our foreign policy. Since 2016 it has been clear that partners and allies elsewhere in the world found the UK's decision to leave the EU difficult to understand. The lack of detail as to what the UK wanted out of leaving the EU or what it meant by the term 'Global Britain' only served to reinforce the idea that the UK was uncertain about the future it saw for itself. There was a view that the Brexit project had come as an unplanned surprise to

UK policy-makers. A sense of frustration from partners was palpable coupled with a sense of drift by those in charge in the UK throughout the years of Brexit stalemate. There was a sense of disbelief that not only was the UK creating more economic barriers but was pursuing a form of Brexit that was considered 'extreme' and much different relationship than other European countries that sat outside the EU.

That has been exacerbated by the extraordinary mess that successive UK Governments have inflicted upon themselves since the EU Referendum. Across Europe and beyond there has been both astonishment and sadness that what had been considered one of the world's more reliable states had got itself into this situation in an entirely avoidable and self-inflicted way.

Within Westminster there was deep frustration and unease. Cross-party efforts and those from devolved administrations to negotiate were rebutted and refused. In part this could have been because any negotiation would have impugned on Westminster's sovereignty in the eyes of Brexiteers and other Westminster politicians. However, it was also because those in charge had no idea what they wanted or what Brexit meant. This certainly appeared to be the case when receiving internal briefings from Ministers and officials in the Brexit team at Number 9 Downing Street. If it was baffling for parliamentarians in the UK then it must have been doubly so for the 27 Member States seeking to comprehend the negotiations. In a recent interview former British Chancellor Philip Hammond said that Theresa May didn't have a clear idea of the kind of relationship we should have with the EU when she became Prime Minister.[257]

Across Europe the UK is now considered an unreliable partner. A British Government Minister stating that the administration was willing to break international law is a comment that took moments to make and from which it will need decades to recover. Rules are important in the relationships between self-respecting democratic and even not so democratic states. We also should not underestimate the damage that has been done by the undermining of the Good Friday peace deal. Then US presidential candidate, Joe Biden's intervention, that any future trade deal 'must be contingent upon respect for the Agreement' was a clear warning that was backed up by Democrats and Republicans. Boris Johnson and the Brexit project had its cheerleaders in the Trump administration who have now left the White House. It is difficult to think of any other administration in the world who now thinks leaving the EU was a good idea.

The UK has never seemed quite so isolated at a time when it needs its friends and allies more than ever. Even within the UK there is a perception of the country's downward international trajectory. A poll by IPSOS MORI in September 2020 showed that less than half of people in the UK, 49 per cent, believe that the country is a force for good in the world. That was down a full ten points on 18 months before.[258]

As part of the UK this leaves Scotland's foreign policy ambitions in a difficult place. Scotland is now a part of a third country in relation to the EU and we will have to work harder than ever before to make our voice heard. Scotland must be clear in what it wants from its international affairs and where it sees itself in the world, now and in the future.

During one of my interviews for this book I spoke to Cat Tully of the School of International Futures who gave evidence during the Foreign Affairs Committee's evidence gathering ahead of the 2014 Referendum. She had told the committee in January 2013 that there would be two differences between Scotland and the UK in terms of foreign policy – 'one of style and the vision of itself'.[259] That vision is still to be developed and she said one of the questions Scotland should be asking itself is: 'what is your story seven generations from now?'

It is a good question and one that we should all be considering. The decisions that we make in the coming months and years will have a profound impact for decades to come. The UK is changing and changing fast, the country that elects a government in 2024 will be very different from the one that went to polls in 2019. Scotland has a strong international brand but how we define ourselves now will be important in the future. There is some immediacy to the question due to Brexit. If we do go down the route of independence, it is worth remembering Professor Malcolm Chalmers words that: 'New states are often defined by decisions made at the start so how you define yourself and getting that right is critical.'

* * *

How a country is seen and perceived by others is an invaluable tool in diplomacy and its soft power is a crucial element in a state unlocking its potential. Over the years, and throughout the interviews that I have held, there has been a broadly held view that Scotland's brand is one of our best national assets, even if it is little understood. Since, and even prior to, devolution successive governments have invested in the nation's brand.

Philip Rycroft said that during his time at the Scotland Office in the 1990s there were efforts for a 'soft projection of Scotland' at trade fairs that he described as being 'slightly hackneyed' with a Minister in a kilt and perhaps a piper but at international events they 'made a splash' and were noticed. There was a strong 'brand recognition' for Scotland even then elsewhere in the world and it was used to sell our products globally as far afield as South Korea and Japan.

The power of our brand is extraordinary given the lack of a Foreign Ministry or global network of embassies. Other non-state actors such as Flanders may have a bigger network but as Professor Nicola McEwen told me: 'Scotland's brand is far in excess of what most other sub-state actors have'. The former Irish Ambassador to the USA, Brendan Scannell, even told me that in his experience Scotland's brand was in some ways better than that of Ireland's. Others may disagree with that assessment but there is agreement that Scotland has a powerful brand.

That brand was developed by Labour administrations at Holyrood not least at Tartan Day events. Amanda Sloat, appointed by Joe Biden as the Senior Director for Europe at the National Security Council, who has viewed Scotland's devolution journey closely said:

> Scots have always been forward leaning in establishing their own brand. You saw it in the creation of Scotland House in Brussels, which brought together businesses and other organisations to share their views with the EU... there was a clear interest in Scotland to present an identity that was distinctive from London.

This was the case under Labour when the Scottish Executive launched the *Best Small Country in the World* campaign, dropped just after the SNP came to power. Personally, I never liked it though I can see why the then Executive wanted to push the brand and the message. That may be because I have never seen Scotland as a small country. As an independent state we would be around mid-ranking in population size in Europe and internationally. The campaign was well-intentioned, and Jack McConnell had also been keen to push a more modern and forward-thinking image for the country after focus group work had illustrated Scotland was seen by some overseas as being a bit backward.

There are other criticisms of the brand. Former Scotland Office Minister Ian Duncan described the national brand as 'not well understood' and that 'we are dealing with shortbread clichés rather than world-leading industries, innovation and research'. Tom Meredith of the HALO Trust said that he would 'love to see the Scottish brand move beyond whisky, golf and Loch Ness'.

I think they are right, but it does give the country a head-start in terms of recognition and a valuable conversation starter when selling the country. I spoke to a former UK Foreign Office Minister and expressed my concerns around the UK Government 'Britain is Great' campaign. Most people I spoke to don't like it and it has been described it as 'toe-curling'. During a meeting of the Foreign Affairs Committee in Labour MP, Ann Clwyd's constituency of Cynon Valley in Wales local small business owners described it as 'unrepresentative' of the UK and a bit 'embarrassing'. The former Minister I spoke to defended the brand and said that there was a 'place for the bearskin hats' simply in terms of recognition and that it was a starting point.

Scotland's brand is evolving as all do over time. International NGOs who bring groups to Scotland report positive feedback. Young leaders say that 'it's different there' and as Craig Oliphant who worked at the Foreign Office for many years points out the hospitality and 'readiness to treat visitors with respect' is very important. During my conversations with those involved in conflict people like David Hamilton, for instance, of Police Scotland came in for praise in setting out the police's work, informed and helped by his experiences in the Bosnian conflict and with Remember Srebrenica Scotland. Others have spent decades building relationships such as former Presiding Officer George Reid, Baroness Elizabeth Smith and Sir Angus Grossart among others.

Those who have worked in conflict note the brand's distinctiveness as having potential especially 'where there is tension'. In the South Caucasus there appears to be good will towards Scotland and everyone I know who worked there picked up on it. In the region 'it doesn't matter' if you are in South Ossetia, Nagorno-Karabakh or in the Scottish pub in Tbilisi, people knew, and liked, Scotland.

Beyond that it has been impressive how many people have spoken of the other aspects of the brand. Sasha Bailie the CEO of Luxinnovation and a former Luxembourg diplomat said: 'Scotland has a unique brand, for example your universities, the energy sector and cities like Glasgow and Edinburgh.' Simon Connell the former Executive Director of Mercy Corps Europe highlighted Scotland's strong brand in areas such as 'medicines, railways and renewables'.

All of these are contributory factors to the brand that goes well beyond tartan and constitutional debates. Former Obama White House Aide Jennifer Erickson said of the Scottish brand, 'there is huge currency Scotland has around the world and a tremendous amount of goodwill that can be claimed in a positive way'.

A recent British Council Report highlighted that Scotland has a strong brand scoring and ranked 16th in the National Brands Index showing that 'Scotland continues to have a strong reputation abroad'.[260] That is important, contributing to the idea of Scotland as an attractive place to work, study and invest. All of that without a Foreign Ministry of Scotland's own.

Developing a distinctive brand is more important now as the UK's is increasingly tarnished. The mess of Brexit and the Johnson Government's disregard for the international rules-based system has not gone unnoticed. Just like in business nations' brands can take decades to build up and remain fragile.

That work is ongoing and though there is a perception the Scottish Government has done well there is more to be done. Professor Anand Menon of King's College London said that Scotland should continue to make itself distinctive from London here and it is important to remember 'that tone matters here' and remember 'humility versus hubris' when dealing with the EU and other international partners.

Scotland can and should set out a distinctive path. That journey is not at an end and will require work and investment. It will also become more difficult as the UK retreats into isolation, for as long as Scotland remains a part of what is seen as a declining and out of touch United Kingdom it will also be affected.

There are lessons to be learned to get the most out of the brand and buy-in from Scots. Sasha Bailie of Luxinnovation described her work in helping Luxembourg re-brand. She told me that some people had perceptions that the Duchy was a 'dodgy financial centre'. She said 'that was never us… but the image sticks'.

In 2012 they started their re-branding exercise. Rather than ask a big PR company to help with those efforts Sasha, a graduate of the University of St Andrews, and her colleagues set to work on asking the people of Luxembourg what they thought of themselves: 'We wanted to grasp the characterisation of Luxembourg, so we asked everyone.'

Over time they spoke to groups of people, young and old, businesses, farmers, NGOs everyone they could find – the 'DNA of Luxembourg'. They found that Luxembourgers saw themselves as 'friends and allies' so that is the vision they took.

> You can't brand and package something until you know what the content is and that comes from every bit of society…. It came from the bottom up, it's authentic.

It is interesting that as Luxembourg wrestled with its brand the answer was to be found at home by including as many people they could in society.

* * *

Throughout my research there has been an understanding of and sympathy for Scotland's foreign policy footprint and the role that we can play. Given its challenges I have been struck by the reluctance of the UK to 'play the whole team' as one senior official from an allied government put it and even consider where the UK could use the power of Scotland's brand as part of a broader UK effort. In some ways it appeared to be more willing to do so before devolution was established than afterwards.

Scotland's foreign policy footprint was an issue that I discussed regularly with politicians and others in Edinburgh, London and Brussels and elsewhere. On 3 December 2018 I secured the 'St Andrews Day' debate on the issue in the House of Commons entitled 'Scotland's

Foreign Policy Footprint'. I may believe in independence, but I was keen to stress in that debate that there was much for the UK to gain in doing more with Scotland's reach:

> it seems apt this evening to reflect on Scotland's place in the world and its foreign policy footprint. I say to the Minister – I know he understands this – that we should have this debate regardless of Scotland's constitutional future. We should have a sensible debate when discussing soft power and the attributes that Scotland brings to the international community. Obviously, he and I will have different views on Scotland's future, and that is entirely legitimate, but I do not think it should take away from our having a sensible dis-cussion of one of the Foreign Office's greatest foreign policy assets—[interruption]. That being, as well as the Minister, Scotland's soft power and the benefit it brings to the Foreign Office's diplomats in doing their work.[261]

Before the debate I sat down with the Foreign Office Minister, Alan Duncan, so that we could try and have a constructive inter-action. The evening however was taken over, once again, by Brexit. It was the last debate of the day and I had to keep speaking until a contempt motion was put down . The motion was put down by me, Keir Starner and colleagues from other parties because of a disagreement over the release of information relating to Brexit.

Alan Duncan was then placed in a similarly difficult position and had to speak until an amendment to our motion had been agreed and submitted by government whips. This meant a much longer debate and without the focus I would have liked. It did allow for the issue to be raised and Alan Duncan was as gracious as he could be. My colleagues and I managed to get several points across albeit in a slightly farcical way due to circumstances entirely outside the Minister's control. Like so many issues that MPs wanted to raise through their brief time in parliament, this was another that was squeezed out as the mess of Brexit sucked the oxygen out of other discussion and debates.

We did air some of the issues and Glasgow-based foreign affairs correspondent David Pratt was able to write ahead of the debate at least:

As Stephen Gethins has made clear in making his case for Monday's Commons debate, it would be so wrong to under-estimate Scotland's global brand contribution to foreign policy over recent years, or indeed its still untapped potential.

What, for example, of the clout and leverage of the Scottish diaspora and its significance in terms of reach into countries across the globe?

What too could be done to further Scotland's example and leadership on climate change as showcased at the Copenhagen Summit?

Even when it comes to the thorny issue of Brexit and our relationship with European neighbours and partners, Scotland's capacity to act as a bridge in the broken relationship between the EU and UK has been overlooked.

Then there is Scotland's unique place as a hub for peace building, bringing people together in places as diverse and far-flung as Syria to the South Caucasus. [262]

Apart from being raised in that debate the UK Government never quite took Scotland's foreign policy potential seriously. I had written to then Foreign Secretary Jeremy Hunt on the issue in October 2018 and received a response that didn't say very much except for a commitment to do better 'by drawing on the breadth of cultural and diplomatic assets that we have at our disposal in the UK'. Alan Duncan's comment in the debate that he struggled to see how Burns' poetry could have an impact on the conflicts of Georgia also missed the point somewhat.

There doesn't appear to have been much progress. In the summer of 2020 the MP for Argyll and Bute, Brendan O'Hara asked a series of questions about events that had taken place to mark St Andrews Day, Burns night as well as Scottish business and culture more generally in the UK's network of embassies.[263] All the FCO was able to come up with were a few embassies flying a Saltire on 30 November, Burns suppers in three embassies and the 'Britain is Great' campaign.

Even for the Foreign Office the efforts seemed poor given the brand and opportunity that Scotland's foreign policy footprint provides the Foreign Office and points to a continued centralisation of foreign policy in Whitehall. As addressed earlier the three embassies mentioned in the parliamentary question that had their Burns suppers in Georgia, Latvia and Hungry were all led by Scottish ambassadors. They appear to have taken some personal initiative to use the event to reach out to stakeholders and highlight the cultural contribution of a major figure in a part of the UK to build international links.

The attitude inside Whitehall appears to be that it is for the Scottish Government to pursue Scotland's foreign policy potential in a very limited sense. There is an attitude that promoting Scotland's national interests is the job of the Scottish Government alone even though the Scotland Act reserves foreign policy to the UK Government. The problem appears to be in Whitehall at a political level with an unwillingness to engage, though one otherwise attentive former Foreign Office Minister recently told me that he had never really thought of the subject.

Others tell a different story. Dan Kenealy, an expert on UK inter-governmental relations and Scotland external relations at the University of Edinburgh, told me that from his conversations 'diplomats in the FCO see the value of Scotland's role but politicians don't'. In other words the problem is a political one and he added 'people in the FCO are open to Scotland playing a bigger role' but there was a refusal at a political level from Government Ministers 'to use all of the assets we have in the UK'.

From conversations with officials in embassies around the world and those who have stepped down from government there is an increasing recognition of the role Scotland could play. Like it or not the enormity of Brexit means that the UK Government needs every foreign policy lever at its disposal. One of the UK's Brexit negotiators once told me:

> If there had been enough political compromise at the Scottish and UK level to find a common interest to get this right. Possibly the Scottish Government could have helped with the May Deal. Scottish Ministers would have added powerfully to the UK team.

Former Conservative MEP, David Campbell Bannerman, also recognised that by highlighting the role that the Scottish diaspora could have played in the USA in securing a trade deal. Instead we saw the power of the Irish diaspora at play in ensuring that respect for the Good Friday Agreement was raised in the US Presidential Election. The UK Government found itself outplayed by Irish diplomacy in Washington DC just as it had been in Brussels.

Any offer to include them would have been impossible for the Scottish Government to have refused. The offer was made to the UK Government to help but turned down. This wouldn't have been an unprecedented move given the role that sub-state actors in Canada and Belgium among other countries play in trade and other international deals. Even as the Brexit negotiations entered their final days in December 2020 the Walloon Minister-President, Elio di Rupo, threatened to veto any deal:

> I will not hesitate to ask my parliament to use its right of veto, as was the case for the #CETA if future trade agreements with the United Kingdom cross the red lines set by my Government.[264]

Hostility in London to Scotland playing a role internationally is nothing new. Henry McLeish talked about finding it difficult to work with a 'Westminster that puts up with devolution' and any help was gained through 'gritted teeth'. He said that his success was due to his personal relationship with Robin Cook, then Foreign Secretary. Even when he engaged with the '40–50 strong' Scottish caucus in Congress the picture of Nancy Pelosi in tartan 'was all to do with an accident' and that 'FCO officials made it very difficult for us'.

Alex Salmond had similar experiences during a British-Irish Council meeting that I attended with him in Jersey in November 2009. There was to be a decision on where the British-Irish Council secretariat would be located. Alex Salmond was determined that it should come to Edinburgh and there was agreement from every delegation including Dublin, Cardiff and both Peter Robinson and Martin McGuiness from Belfast as well as the Channel Islands and Isle of Man.

Scotland was seen as 'neutral-ground' and it should have been a straight forward decision. Despite being in a minority of one the

UK Government represented by Peter Hain vetoed the idea at that Summit with officials saying privately that they did not want to give the Scots a victory. It damaged the UK's reputation and the secretariat came to Edinburgh in the end anyway.

* * *

The Scottish Government has been developing its brand and relationships with international actors over the past few years with successive administrations making use of Scotland's global reach and soft power potential. A recent British Council Report highlighted Scotland's work in this area and use of 'para-diplomacy'.

> Scotland's most useful way to pursue objectives beyond its borders is to utilise the full spectrum of soft power. Successive Scottish governments have worked effectively to use the resources at their disposal to engage globally...
>
> Soft power is ideally suited to Scotland's unique status as a devolved authority that has many features of an independent country, though remains within the structure of the United Kingdom.[265]

Scotland has used that soft power potential in areas such as climate justice, peace-building, trade and EU engagement among others. This has been pursued by successive First Ministers during their periods of office. SNP First Ministers have obviously seen the need for a distinctive foreign policy but so too have pro-Union First Ministers. Speaking at an Institute for Government event in 2018 Jack McConnell underlined the importance of that international approach especially when there was a discussion and debate over whether we should have a Scottish Parliament and no certainty that devolution would last:

> I wanted us to be proactive outside Scotland. I wanted the Scottish Parliament and Scottish Government to be engaged. Partly because it was important for Scotland to not become insular just because we had got a Scottish Parliament. While there were big problems to deal with at home, I felt the best of Scotland over the centuries had been outward looking and engaged internationally, and I thought we should do that.[266]

Since that time the Scottish Government has taken that forward with an external engagement policy with some success. There has been work areas as diverse as South Asia, the USA and Japan.

The different approaches were on display during the visit to Beijing in 2017 with David Lidington and the cross-party group. There were plenty of formal events and a lot of sitting in neat rows listening to speeches. One of my days in Beijing coincided with the First Minister's visit to the city. That evening I joined a Scottish Government reception to say hello to colleagues. The contrast between the formal UK events and the Scottish Government event was enormous. After days of formal structured meetings, I was thrown into an evening of Scottish ballet with an eastern twist, meeting Chinese people marketing whisky fully dressed in tartan and watching university representatives work the room while eating Scottish seafood. The benefits of not being restricted by too much diplomatic protocol or big power status was apparent and the Scots were taking full advantage.

Cat Tully told me that 'Scotland and Wales have been creative because they don't have power over foreign policy'. That will become even more important as the UK moves away from the EU with Scotland having to work harder as a part of a country with fewer ties to the EU institutions. Scotland will have to be even more inventive in its international engagement as it lacks even the limited means for institutional engagement it enjoyed previously as part of the EU.

It will require investment at a time when resources are stretched and there has rightly been a focus on dealing with the crisis of Covid-19 as well as the UK leaving the EU and the economic consequences of both. If Scotland is to maintain its links there will have to be an increased presence in Brussels, other EU capitals and around the world.

Political engagement is also important. Scottish politicians are often criticised for travelling but it is and should be part of the job. There is a place for scrutiny and responsible use of public funds but criticising travel for the sake of it is short-sighted. Travel is exhausting and can take you away from home but in an inter-connected world international engagement should be a part of a Minister's role, it certainly is elsewhere in Europe where states have built and maintain relationships across borders.

In Brussels there will have to be a focus on maintaining and building relationships. Luxembourg's Sasha Bailie's advice for Scotland is that:

> You need to remain in the loop in Brussels, the human relationships are very important... You have to be a facilitator and bridge-builder, that is the lesson that Luxembourg has learned.

Others have made the same observations. Professor Nicola McEwen has said that we need to look at how this is done in the future and that at times she says 'the Scottish Government doesn't always keep itself in the loop' even though there is a big team it is 'under-resourced' in London, and in Brussels. The Brussels office has been focused more on 'raising awareness of Scotland and keeping abreast of EU affairs, rather than influencing EU policy'.

The appointment of experienced officials and those with diplomatic experience in Dublin, Brussels and Edinburgh is helpful and won praise from friends overseas but there is a question over whether it is enough to meet the challenges ahead. Michael Russell has told me that the Scottish Government is looking to bring in more expertise. It is a government that is building for independence and the responsibilities around foreign affairs that come with that. That means the Scottish Government beefing up diplomatic and political experience and presence.

* * *

Responsibility for creating a successful approach in building international outreach does not just lie with government and it is important that other parts of Scotland are included in building the 'team'. There is a strong role that other actors can play.

The education sector already has a strong track record in building partnerships and links around the world. As the British Council Report found:

> Education is a powerful tool that Scotland has leveraged to engage with international partners, as seen in its prominence in the Scotland is Now campaign. Study in Scotland

is a targeted campaign that promotes students. Beyond its remarkable higher education standards, Study in Scotland promotes the wider experience of student life in Scotland, and acts as the one-stop information centre for interested applicants.[267]

There was also praise for the engagement between cities in Scotland. In the aftermath of the Second World War, German mayors worked to rebuild relationships with city twinning across Europe. That has grown and I can remember learning about Aschaffenburg in Germany when I was younger, meeting the Mayor of Haikou in China and trying out my French with pupils from Cognac who visited Perth. As the Berlin Wall fell students from Perth's twin town Pskov in Russia took part in a Peace Child play bringing together young people from around the world in May 1991.

It goes beyond twinning to major economic development and cities like Dundee, Aberdeen, Edinburgh and Glasgow have world brands they should have civic pride in. They even had a role to play and their say in international affairs such as the fight against apartheid. Nelson Mandela visited Glasgow in 1993 to thank the city for its leadership and support that it provided to the anti-apartheid movement. Mandela was given the freedom of the city in 1981 well before his release and in opposition to fashionable opinion as campaigner Brian Filling put it. In his speech Nelson Mandela told Glaswegians about the difference they had made:

> While we were physically denied our freedom in the country of our birth, a city 6,000 miles away, and as renowned as Glasgow, refused to accept the legitimacy of the apartheid system, and declared us to be free.[268]

Culture has a role to play as has been seen in the Edinburgh festivals that Jonathan Cohen highlighted as part of Scotland's success in bringing people together. As one academic highlighted to me, 'ideas about diplomacy are changing' and 'the Scottish Government seem to get it'. In Moscow I watched musicians brought from the UK to Russia to perform and so maintain cultural links when political connections were at another low. Those efforts at cultural diplomacy were thanks to the work of the excellent British Council officials working with the Embassy there.

Cultural diplomacy has an important role to play, it is a means of building bridges and maintaining connections that we need. Mark Muller Stuart said of Scotland's potential:

> its cultural festivals, soft power, legal and educational institutions, countryside and castles, provide the perfect backdrop for cultural diplomacy and engagement with international civil society.[269]

Similarly, with sports where Scotland has a global reach and recognition, even if the national football team don't always match that international excellence on the field that many of us would like to see. However Scotland's recent qualification for the 2021 European Championship will be a great opportunity for Scots. In 2014 Scotland's success in hosting the Commonwealth games was a tremendous showcase for the country around the world.

Business leaders such as financier Sir Angus Grossart and energy entrepreneur Sir Ian Wood have also used Scotland's global footprint. These businesses have global connections and are firmly rooted in Scotland. Environmental NGOs have built links throughout the world with their work on diversity and climate change among others as have peace-building NGOs working in areas affected by conflict been developing their Scottish footprint. COP26 will be yet another opportunity for a city with a global brand, Glasgow, and Scotland itself to build on their international reputations.

Scotland's foreign policy is and should be a team effort. That does not mean that we should all have the same focus, be striving for the same goals or always be in agreement with each other but it is an important network that has a vested interest in the brand and the country's soft power potential.

* * *

In striving to build our foreign policy footprint and especially soft power it is important to draw lessons from others. Ireland put a huge amount of effort into winning its place on the UN Security Council. A Team Ireland approach was developed and the lessons it learned are well worth considering. To gain enough support to get onto the Security Council the Irish had to build connections and support across the world. All 192 UN members were contacted by either the Taoiseach (Prime Minister), Tánaiste (Deputy Prime Minister) or President themselves and they also drafted the star power of pop star Bono.

The Irish drew on every resource in their extensive soft power armoury. Sometimes that was down to some politics where Irish support for the two-state solution to the Israel/Palestine conflict and the Middle East peace process was important. In Africa its record on sustainable development and peacekeeping won backers. In South America a connection with independence movements and an emotional connection with island nations – and even a night out in Co. Cork with a former Foreign Minister of Kiribati involving a sing-along – helped secure votes. The Irish were able to use the full diplomatic muscle at their disposal to become 'very relatable' to other countries with the Irish Times reporting that those nations 'saw in Ireland's story a version of their own'.[270]

That soft power and how a country is portrayed is incredibly important and the Irish have used their clout fully. The other winner of a spot on the UN Security Council was another one of our neighbours, Norway. Again, it sees its role in international organisations as being part of its identity both at a global level and how it interacts with its neighbours where the Nordics 'pool their influence for common gain' as SNP MP Martin Docherty-Hughes put it. This idea is of 'smart-state' diplomacy where both Ireland and Norway present themselves as 'honest brokers'.

Canada lost out in its bid to these two countries with a leading security expert and Canadian, Steve Saideman, tweeting: 'even if Canada did everything right, it started late and faced two really terrific countries that do their foreign policy really well'.[271]

Luxembourgers know from long experience that they cannot compete with the big states. And although it is more difficult to draw parallels with Luxembourg than say Ireland or Norway there are lessons that we can take from them as well. The country takes advantage of not being perceived as a threat and as 'non-competitive' taking the role of a 'neutral coordinator'. Community connectivity is also important given the small size of the country with a smaller bureaucracy and civil society, so connections can be more informal. This is something that those who have worked in London will often remark upon when they come to Scotland where it is easier to connect given the more manageable size of our networks.[272]

Cat Tully also pointed out that Costa Rica punches above its weight because of its own community connectivity. The vision of the future of Costa Rica's identity and role in the world is held collectively by the public and wider community rather than just government elites.

Critical to all of this is the importance of inter-connectivity, the rule of law and the idea of pooling and sharing sovereignty to all these successful small and medium-sized states. In the immediate aftermath of Ireland winning its seat on the UN Security Council in June 2020 then Foreign Minister Simon Coveney made a short statement welcoming the historic moment. He summed up how Ireland sees itself in the world and his words are worth considering:

> Why does it matter that our small country sits on the UN Security Council? I have heard the criticism the problems are too big and big states won't listen. To those people I point out that in the last six months the world has been threatened by a virus that knows no nationality, no borders and respect no superpower. Countries are fighting back but we don't yet have a medicine. The only thing we have is shared knowledge. We have knowledge on how to slow the spread and how to prevent infection. No one country on earth will stop coronavirus. Just like no one country on earth will counter climate change or hunger or aids or poverty or gender inequality or deliver peace in conflict zones. Our belief in multilateralism is a cornerstone of Irish foreign policy. Together we are stronger. The voice of small countries also provide global solutions.[273]

That idea of working together stands in stark contrast to the UK that is emerging from Brexit. That unilateralist approach is the opposite of the way that Scotland's foreign policy and international engagement needs to evolve. It is the reason that the *acquis communitaire* or common rules agreed by the EU's Member States are so important. Small, and medium-sized, members see commonly agreed rules as a means of protecting themselves through international law and the rule of law. It is why the Baltic states see membership of the EU as a means of protecting their democracy and strengthening their sovereignty. At its annual meeting of ambassadors from around the world, Lithuanian Foreign Minister, Linas Linkkevičius, talked about membership of the EU and NATO being an important part of the country's independence journey telling his colleagues:

> I believe that a world order based on the rule of law and democracy is our state's fundamental interest. It is much more beneficial than the one based on the rule of the 'law of the jungle'.[274]

There are some who have even argued in the past that we are now in a period of 'post sovereign' states in Europe and even that 'the era of absolute state sovereignty had ended'.[275] I am not sure that is correct since that idea of state sovereignty is so central to the EU treaties and why the idea of the UK negotiating with its 'sovereign equal' the EU was so ridiculed. As the Spanish Minister for Foreign Affairs, the EU and Cooperation told *Sky News* on 13 December 2020 in relations to the ongoing negotiations with the UK: 'A trade deal is not made to assert our independence but to manage our interdependence.'

There is recognition of the centrality of being a good global citizen and operating in an international arena where compromise and the pooling and sharing of sovereignty is so important. Rasmus Helveg Petersen said, 'the grand foreign policy strategy of Denmark is to have a rules-based system'. Here our neighbours to the north, east and west are closer to us in outlook than those to the south. Speaking at the University of Georgetown, Washington DC in 2019 Nicola Sturgeon said:

> by and large, people in Scotland and this is perhaps in contrast with people elsewhere in the UK, don't really see membership of the European Union as a threat to our own national sovereignty.[276]

That may be uncontroversial for a First Minister to say but one can no longer imagine a British Prime Minister agreeing. Within the UK there is a difference in how we see ourselves in the world coupled with different ideas of sovereignty. That does demand a greater understanding of foreign affairs and the views of others in our debate. One of the great failures of the Brexit debate was in just how absent an understanding of the EU was and even a serious attempt to understand the EU's point of view. Scotland cannot afford to make the same mistakes. It is important that we understand and debate our place in the world and what is driving Brexit in our biggest neighbour so that we understand their ambitions and ensure mistakes are not repeated.

* * *

The UK's decision to leave the European Union has been a profoundly impactful experience in the UK. For the first time many Scots are considering independence who would have steadfastly rejected it in the past. The issue of Scotland's place in the world may have been little explored in 2014 but will be central to any future vote. It changes the goalposts for everyone engaged in the constitutional debate. Although it brings fresh opportunities there are also hard questions to be answered over our relationship with the rest of the United Kingdom.

There is also a challenge for those who back the Union. The option of remaining in the United Kingdom leaves even harder questions with how we conduct ourselves internally. The UK has become more isolated internationally and more centralised domestically as a result of leaving the EU and the direction of politics since. There is no status quo option for Scotland anymore.

This is a question that cannot be ducked. The UK is changing fast and will continue to change rapidly as Britain in the EU fades further from memory. Any decision on Scotland's future will not be on the same basis as 2014 and any future decision would result in different outcomes. Remaining part of a post-Brexit UK would be different than in 2014 as would independence with the UK now outside the EU.

One former official who was an enthusiastic supporter of the Union previously and remained so at time of writing remains so said:

> Brexit is a deeply rupturing experience that changes things. With so many of the attributes of statehood already built into the Union it isn't a huge leap of imagination to see Scotland as a full Member State [of the EU].

Our debate is little understood and maybe the time has come for more investment in our foreign policy. On the one hand Scotland has as much to gain as our neighbours have from independence and the benefits that might bring. Supporters of the Union may consider how they can gain from Scotland having greater clout and as former British Ambassador Alyson Bailes put it, the UK is 'letting its right hand and left hand reach out separately'.[277]

There is a need to deepen our understanding around our foreign policy footprint in Scotland, across the political divide. There have been short comings in all parties, and we need to think about where we sit in the world. Scotland's international footprint cannot be wished away nor can it assumed to be an automatic success.

Other sub-state actors have their own institutes for both peace and international affairs for example. It is time to try and do something similar in Scotland with the Scottish Global Forum providing a useful forerunner ahead of the 2014 Referendum. This is not happening in a vacuum and smart people are giving the subject plenty of thought. The Scottish Government should consider how it can develop that agenda internally and more widely across the country. Similarly, the UK needs to consider, if it wants Scotland to remain, how it can respond to Scotland's undoubted potential in international affairs and the goodwill it has generated.

I started this book looking at lessons from history and we now sit at another historic crossroads. That means thinking beyond the present and perceived wisdom about our place in the world. As Professor Steve Murdoch of the University of St Andrews told me: 'At different times Scotland has had a relationship with so many countries that can be tapped into from zero. It comes and goes.'

In other words the status quo does not last for long and nations decide where they feel most comfortable in the world around them on an ongoing basis. We are at the end of a chapter of history and we don't know what the next few years will bring. That will be up to us and the decisions we make in the coming months and years ahead.

Index

Endnotes

1   MacCormick v. Lord Advocate (1953) sc 396 – Court of Session (on appeal)

2   Wintour, Patrick, 'May "Did Not Understand EU When She Triggered Brexit"', *The Guardian*, 5 March 2019

3   Muller Stuart, Mark, 'Using Culture and Scotland's Soft Power to Help to Resolve Conflict', speech to the Royal Society of Arts, 24 November 2017

4   dictionary.cambridge.org/dictionary/english/foreign-policy

5   Hansard, House of Commons, 1 July 2020

6   Andrews, Kieran, 'Anger Over Johnson's "No Border" Blunder', *The Times*, 2 July 2020

7   Beard, Mary, *SPQR: A History of Ancient Rome*, Profile Books Ltd, 2015

8   Webb, Jim, *Born Fighting: How the Scots-Irish Shaped America*, Broadway, 2005

9   MacNeill, Duncan H, *The Scottish Realm: An Approach to Political and Constitutional History of Scotland*, A&J Donaldson Ltd, 1947

10   For more reading on this see Steven Douglas Keith, 'The Origins of Scotland and Where its People Came From', History is Now Magazine blog, 10 March 2019

11   Kay, Billy, 'The Declaration of Arbroath', BBC Radio Scotland, 11 April 2020

12   Murray, David, *The First Nation in Europe: A Portrait of Scotland the Scots*, Pall Mall Press, 1960

13   www.royal.uk/order-thistle – It remains the highest order in Scotland although the website does mention that the Order may have been founded by James III who reigned between 1488 and 1513

14   Lynch, Michael *Scotland: A New History*, Pimlico, 1992

15   Ditchburn, David and MacDonald, Alistair J, 'Medieval Scotland 1100–1560' in Houston, RA and Knox, WWJ (eds), *History of Scotland*, Penguin, 2002

16   Ian Duncan passed me a fabulous book by Thomas Moncrieff, *The Ancient Alliance Between the French and Scots and the Privileges of the*

Scots in France, taken from the 'Original Records of the Kingdom of France' and originally printed by W Cheyne, 1751

17 Senate motion establishing Tartan Day agreed on 20 March 1998 – www.congress.gov/bill/105th-congress/senate-resolution/155/text

18 Fleming, Alexander and Mason, Roger, *Scotland the Flemish People*, Birlinn, 2019

19 Church and Kirk, like so many Dutch words, is of course the same in Scots

20 More information can be found on the museum's website is – www.museumveere.nl/welcome-to-museum-veere/

21 See Dundee City archives – www.fdca.org.uk/Veere_Staple.html

22 The Veere archivist, Peter Blom, gave a fascinating talk on the files that can be found on the Dundee City Archives website – www.fdca.org.uk/pdf%20files/veere_13.pdf

23 'Scotland's Intercourse with Northern Europe', *Northern Notes and Queries*, Edinburgh University Press, Vol. 4, No. 16, pp.178–80

24 The Story of the Schottentor, 19 June 2019, Secret Vienna Walking Tours website – www.secretvienna.org

25 Murdoch, Steve, Chapter 8 in Harris, Bob and MacDonald, Alan, *Scotland and Europe: The Making and Unmaking of a Nation 1100–1707*: Vol. 2, Edinburgh University Press, 2012

26 ibid.

27 For further reading and more fascinating tales of the influence of Scots read Steve Murdoch who teaches at the University of St Andrews and Billy Kay especially *The Scottish World: A Journey Into the Scottish Diaspora*, Mainstream Publishing, 2008

28 Website of the Royal Family – www.royal.uk/james-iv-r1488-1513

29 Mapstone, Professor Sally, Installation Address, 29 November 2016

30 Church of Scotland Report of the Church and Nation Committee to the 1996 General Assembly.

31 Encyclical of Pope Leo XIII on the Church in Scotland given at St Peter's Rome, 25 July 1898 – www. cotlan.va

32 Norwich, John Julius, *The Popes*, Vintage, 2011

33 Ditchburn, David and MacDonald, Alistair J, 'Medieval Scotland 1100–1560' in Houston, RA and Knox, WWJ (eds), *History of Scotland*, Penguin, 2002

34 ibid.

35 Murdoch, Steve, Chapter 8 in Harris, Bob and MacDonald, Alan, *Scotland and Europe: The Making and Unmaking of a Nation 1100–1707*: Vol. 2, Edinburgh University Press, 2012

36 BBC Bitesize, The Treaty of Edinburgh, 1560

37 Murdoch, Steve, Chapter 8 in Harris, Bob and MacDonald, Alan, *Scotland and Europe: The Making and Unmaking of a Nation 1100–1707*: Vol. 2, Edinburgh University Press, 2012

38 For further reading see the BBC website – www.bbc.co.uk/history/british/civil_war_revolution/cotland_darien_01.Shtml

39 Henderson Scott, Paul, *The Union of 1707*, The Saltire Society, 2006

40 Hart Dyke, Tom and Winder, Paul, *The Cloud Garden*, Bantam, 2003

41 Kay, Billy, 'The Declaration of Arbroath', BBC Radio Scotland, 11 April 2020

42 See Scottish Review of Books, 'Voltaire versus Lord Kames and the Need for a Soundbite', 19 June 2019

43 MacKay, Neil, 'US Racism Demands Scotland Reflects on its Shameful Past of White Supremacy', *The Herald*, 4 June 2020

44 Alex Massie, column, *The Times*, 9 June 2020

45 Devine, Tom, 'If We Erase the Past How Can We Ever Learn From It', *Daily Mail*, 9 June 2020

46 Ewing, Winnie, *Stop the World: The Autobiography of Winnie Ewing*, Birlinn, 2004

47 Fenby, Jonathan, *The General: Charles de Gaulle and the France He Saved*, Simon & Schuster, 2010

48 Perth & Kinross Council – Tributes paid to Heroes of St Valery (pkc.gov.uk)

49 Murphy, Sean, 'The Auld Alliance', *The Scotsman*, 9 January 2015

50 Interview with Professor Steve Murdoch

51 'The History of Robert Burns Statues Around the World', *The Scotsman*, 21 January 2016

52 Strachan, Graeme, 'Remembering the Pulitzer Prize Winner Whose Lifelong Love Affair with Dundee United Had a Happy Ending', *The Courier*, 22 February 2020

53 Hastings, Max, 'Max Hastings on a New Method of Global Dominance; The Way to Influence the World is With Fizzy Drinks and Pop Music, Not Military Might', review of *Soft Power* by Robert Winder, *Sunday Times*, 2 August 2020

54 Heather, Alistair, 'Why the Finns Believe Scotland Could Become Nordic Nation Number Six', *The Scotsman*, 17 May 2020

55 Twitter, @IlvesToomas, 24 January 2021

56 *The Scottish Diaspora and Diaspora Strategy: Insights and Lessons from Ireland*, Scottish Government, 29 May 2009

57 'The Scottish Diaspora: How Scots Spread Across the Globe', *The Scotsman*, 25 January 2016

58 Herman, Arthur, *The Scottish Enlightenment: The Scots Invention of the Modern World*, Harper Collins, 2003

59 Hesse, David, *Warrior Dreams: Playing Scotsmen in Mainland Europe*, Manchester University Press, 2014

60 Damer, S, *The Scottish Dreamscape*, Edinburgh University Press, 2017

61 'The US Presidents With the Strongest Scottish Roots', *The Scotsman*, 5 March 2016

62 Chicago Scots website – www.chicagoscots.org/scottishamericanhalloffame

63 Twitter feed of CG Ireland Atlanta, @IrelandAtlanta, 3 December 2020

64 Scottish Government website – www.scotland.org/about-scotland/scotland-around-the-world

65 Hansard, House of Commons, Canada, 25 January 2021

66 Ferguson, Niall, *Empire: How Britain Made the Modern World*, Penguin Books, 2004

67 Kay, Billy, *The Scottish World: A Journey into the Scottish Diaspora*, Mainstream Publishing, 2008

68 Argentinian Football Association website – www.afa.com.ar/es/pages/historia

69 Barry, Ellen, 'Barriers That Are Steep and Linguistic', *New York Times*, 24 August 2008

70 For more on the region see Tom de Waal, *The Caucasus: An Introduction*, Oxford University Press, 2010

71 Ascherson, Neal, *Black Sea*, Vintage, 1996

72 McCarthy, Angela and MacKenzie, John, *Global Migrations: The Scottish Diaspora Since 1600*, Edinburgh University Press, 2016

73 ibid.

74 At 17.5 Million Indian Diaspora is the Largest in the World: UN Report, *The Economic Times*, 18 September 2019

75 Dáil Éireann debate, 28 June 1963 – www.oireachtas.ie/en/debates/debate/dail/1963-06-28/2/

76 'How Brexit is Leading a Resurgent Irish American Influence in US Politics', *The Conversation*, 6 August 2019

77 Irish Department of Foreign Affairs website, the Irish Abroad – www.dfa. ie/our-role-policies/the-irish-abroad/

78 Foreign Affairs Committee Written Evidence, *Foreign Policy Considerations for the UK and Scotland in the Event of Scotland Becoming an Independent Country*, April 2013

79 Irish Department of Foreign Affairs, Global Irish – www.dfa.ie/ global-irish/consultations/

80 Irish Department of Foreign Affairs press release, 'Colm Brophy TD, appointed as Minister for Overseas Development Aid and Diaspora', 2 July 2020

81 'How Ireland Gets its Way: An Unlikely Diplomatic Superpower', *The Economist*, 17 July 2020

82 'How Brexit is Leading a Resurgent Irish American Influence in US Politics', *The Conversation*, 6 August 2019

83 Giragosian, Richard, *Armenia's Diaspora: Helpful Advantage or Harmful Adversary?*, The Foreign Policy Centre, 21 March 2017

84 'France Marks First National Commemoration of Armenian Genocide', *France 24*, 24 April 2019

85 Haltiwanger, John, 'Trump's White House Press Secretary Invoked the "Armenian Genocide", But the US Government Has Never Officially Recognized it and This Could Anger Turkey', *Business Insider*, 7 July 2020

86 Giragosian, Richard, *Armenia's Diaspora: Helpful Advantage or Harmful Adversary?*, The Foreign Policy Centre, 21 March 2017

87 Salam, Yasmine, Radnofsky, Caroline and Gostanian, Ali, 'Armenian Americans Build Support for Distant Homeland as Fragile Peace Holds in Nagorno-Karabakh', NBC News, 16 November 2020

88 Sesin, Carmen, 'Trump Cultivated the Latino Vote in Florida and it Paid Off', NBC News, 4 November 2020

89 Woollacott, Martin, 'One in Six Iraqis Are in Exile and They Want This War', *The Guardian*, 16 August 2002

90 Vertovec, Steve, *The Political Importance of Diasporas*, Migration Policy Institute, 1 June 2005

91 Kuznetsov, Yuri, 'Leveraging Diasporas of Talent: Towards a New Policy Agenda' in Kuznetsov, Yuri (ed), *Diaspora Networks and the*

International Migration of Skills: How Countries Can Draw on Their Talent Abroad, World Bank Institute, 2006

92 Ministry of Education and Culture, Estonia – www.meis.ee/en/

93 Lithuania Ministry of Foreign Affairs press release, 'Lithuania's Foreign Ministry is Committed to its "Global Lithuanian" Programme', 13 October 2012

94 Birka, Leva, *Can Return Migration Revitalize the Baltics? Estonia, Latvia, and Lithuania Engage Their Diasporas, with Mixed Results*, Migration Policy Institute, 8 May 2019

95 Vertovec, Steven, *The Political Importance of Diasporas,* Migration Policy Institute, 1 June 2005

96 Croatian Parliament website – www.sabor.hr/en/mps/constituencies

97 Tsourapas, Gerasimos, *A Tightening Grip Abroad: Authoritarian Regimes Target Their Emigrant and Diaspora Communities*, Migration Policy Institute, 22 August 2019

98 Ascherson, Neal, *Black Sea,* Vintage, 1996

99 MacRae, Mairi and Wight, Martin, 'A Model Diaspora Network: The Origin and Evolution of GlobalScot' in Kuznetsov, Yuri (ed), *Diaspora Networks and the International Migration of Skills: How Countries Can Draw on Their Talent Abroad,* World Bank Institute, 2006

100 Mullin, Roger and Thomson, Michelle, *Scottish Business and International Trade – Perceptions of the Scottish Business Diaspora,* Momentous Change Ltd, January 2020

101 MacRae, Mairi and Wight, Martin, 'A Model Diaspora Network: The Origin and Evolution of GlobalScot' in Kuznetsov, Yuri (ed), *Diaspora Networks and the International Migration of Skills: How Countries Can Draw on Their Talent Abroad,* World Bank Institute, 2006

102 Mullin, Roger and Thomson, Michelle, *Scottish Business and International Trade – Perceptions of the Scottish Business Diaspora,* Momentous Change Ltd, January 2020

103 Ancien, Dr Delphine, Boyle, Prof. Mark and Kitchin, Prof. Rob, *The Scottish Diaspora and Diaspora Strategy: Insights and Lessons from Ireland*, Scottish Government, 2009

104 Full text of the response:

Written Parliamentary Question 72209: To ask the Secretary of State for Foreign and Commonwealth Affairs, what events took place in UK (a) embassies and (b) other diplomatic missions to mark St Andrews Day in 2019. (72209) – Tabled on: 10 July 2020

This question was grouped with the following question(s) for answer:
To ask the Secretary of State for Foreign and Commonwealth Affairs, what events took place in (a) embassies and (b) other diplomatic missions to mark Burns Night in (i) 2019 and (ii) 2020. (72210) Tabled on: 10 July 2020
To ask the Secretary of State for Foreign and Commonwealth Affairs, what events were hosted in UK (a) embassies and (b) other diplomatic missions to promote Scottish (i) business and (ii) culture in the last 12 months. (72211) Tabled on: 10 July 2020
Answer:
Nigel Adams:

It is important for the FCO overseas network to promote the interests and diversity of the whole of the UK to other countries – this includes promoting Scotland at events hosted to mark St Andrew's Day and Burns Night.

We do not hold a central log of all the events hosted across the world, but some examples for Burns Night include our Ambassadors in Latvia, Hungary and Georgia each hosting a Burns Night supper with key stakeholders to promote Scottish culture and trade. Others promoted St Andrew's Day on social media and flew the Saltire on the day itself.

Furthermore, the GREAT marketing campaign also promotes Scottish business and culture throughout the world. The GREAT Challenge Fund is run from the FCO to enable Posts to deliver impactful GREAT activity overseas. Last financial year, there were over 40 projects promoting the devolved nations including: Bookfest International Fair in Bucharest featuring elements of Scottish literature and a Higher Education partnership in Germany promoting the University of Aberdeen and Scottish primary and secondary schools.

The answer was submitted on 16 Jul 2020

105 Ewing, Winnie, *Stop the World: The Autobiography of Winnie Ewing*, Birlinn, 2004

106 Devine, Tom, 'Leading Historian Says Scots Should be Proud of our Mongrel Nation', *Daily Record*, 6 September 2015

107 Keane, Kevin, 'Polish Election Fever Hits Fife', BBC Scotland, 30 September 2007

108 Knox, John, 'Holyrood Has its Say on Iraq', BBC Scotland, 16 January 2003

109 McConnell, Jack, interview, Institute for Government, 6 September 2018

110 External Affairs Directorate, Scottish Government – www.gov.scot/about/how-government-is-run/directorates/external-affairs-directorate/

111 For more information see – www.gov.scot/international/

112 Adam Forrest, '"Grotesquely Tone Deaf": Tory Minister Lambasted for Asking Boris Johnson to Spend Aid Money on New Royal Yachts, *The Independent*, 18 June 2020

113 Hansard, House of Commons Debate on the Royal Yacht Britannia, 11 October 2016

114 'Salmond Will Attend Climate Talks', BBC News, 11 December 2009

115 'Alex Salmond's Whisky Warning to World Leaders in Copenhagen', *The Guardian*, 15 December 2009

116 Maldives Government notice from 15 December 2009 – www.presidency.gov.mv/Press/Article/781

117 Scottish Parliament Information Centre Report, *Cancún: UN Climate Negotiations*, 29 November 2010

118 25 October 2011 – www.youtube.com/watch?v=pn54FI2JBXQ

119 Cheam, Jessica, 'First Minister of Scotland Alex Salmond Stepped Up to Formally Announce Signing a Joint Statement on Co-operation with President Nasheed of the Maldives', *Eco-Business*, 15 December 2009

120 Alex Salmond speech to the Communist Party School of China, December 2011 –www.mrfcj.org/pdf/Speech_to_Communist_Party_Central_School-_Alex_Salmond_First_Minister_Scotland.pdf

121 'Scotland Announces "Climate Justice" Fund for the World's Poorest', *The Guardian*, 6 June 2012

122 WWF Scotland: Ten Years of Scottish Climate Action – www.wwf.org.uk/updates/10-years-scottish-climate-action

123 Renewable Energy Facts & Statistics | Scottish Renewables – www.scottish renewables.com

124 Scottish Government Greenhouse Gas Emissions 2018: estimates, 16 June 2020

125 The author writes about 'Regional Governments' and that would mean sub-state actors including the Scottish Government. Lecours, André, *Political Issues of Paradiplomacy: Lessons from the Developed World*, Netherlands Institute of International Relations 'Clingendael', 1 December 2008

126 Denmark's Ministry of Foreign Affairs – www.um.dk/en/foreign-policy/greenland-and-the-faroe-islands/

127 For more information see Visit the Faroes website – www.
visitfaroeislands.com/

128 The Faroese Government has an extensive part of its website in
English setting its responsibilities and activities. It even has the contact
email and telephone numbers of key officials – www.government.fo/en/
foreign-relations/the-faroe-islands-in-the-international-community/

129 Foreign Affairs Committee oral evidence, 15 January 2013

130 See Greenlandic Government website – www.naalakkersuisut.
gl/en/Naalakkersuisut/Departments/Udenrigsanliggende/
Om-Udenrigsanliggender/Ansvarsomraader

131 Pengelly, Martin, 'Trump Confirms He is Attempting to Buy Greenland',
The Guardian, 18 August 2019

132 See note – www.government.fo/en/foreign-relations/the-faroe-islands-
in-the-international-community/

133 For further information see Pram Gad, Ulrik, 'Could a "Reverse
Greenland" Keep Scotland and Northern Ireland in the EU', EUROPP,
London School of Economics blog, 7 July 2016

134 Submission by the Isle of Man Government to the House of Commons
Foreign Affairs Committee, August 2016

135 Government of Jersey website – www.gov.je

136 Jersey Overseas Aid – www.joa.je

137 Website for the states of Guernsey – www.gov.gg

138 Salamone, Anthony, report to Scottish Parliament Europe Committee,
*Scotland's Engagement with the European Union – Insights from Third
Countries and Regions*, October 2019 on behalf of the Scottish Centre on
European Relations

139 ibid.

140 Flanders, Department of Foreign Affairs countries and regions – www.
fdfa.be/en/diplomacy

141 From – www.fdfa.be/en

142 Flemish Government press release, 'Pleased With Brexit Fund in EU
Budget Package', 21 July 2020

143 The Fish Site, UK *Government Accused of Ignoring Fishing Industry*, 5
May 2010

144 Criekemanns, Davd, discussion papers in *Diplomacy, Foreign Policy and
Diplomacy in the Belgian Regions: Flanders and Walloonia*, Netherlands
Institute of International Relations, Clingendael, March 2010

145 For more information – www.fdfa.be/en/csg

146 McClory, Jonathan, *Gauging International Perceptions: Scotland and Soft Power*, Portland for the British Council Scotland, 2020

147 Québec's International Policy – www.quebec.ca/en/government/policies-orientations/quebec-international-policy/

148 ibid.

149 Salamone, Anthony, Report to Scottish Parliament Europe Committee, *Scotland's Engagement with the European Union – Insights from Third Countries and Regions*, October 2019 on behalf of the Scottish Centre on European Relations

150 ibid., p. 27

151 McFadden, Jean and McFadzean, Dale, 'Structure of Government in the UK', *Scottish Administrative Law Essentials*, Edinburgh University Press, 2006), pp. 19–24

152 Russell, Rachel, 'Sturgeon Undermining Brexit Talks by Forcing Scottish Fishermen Back Into Hated EU Policy', *Daily Express*, 2 December 2020

153 UK in a Changing Europe, Brexit Witness Archive – www.ukandeu.ac.uk/brexit-witness-archive

154 Government of Ireland – www.ireland.ie/media/ireland/stories/globaldiaspora/Global-Ireland-in-English.pdf

155 Zeffman, Henry, 'What Happens to Britain's "Special Relationship", If Joe Biden Becomes US President', *The Times*, 6 July 2020

156 Section 7.1 Church of Scotland Report of the Church and Nation Committee to the 1996 General Assembly

157 Donald Dewar's speech at the opening of the Scottish Parliament, 1 July 1999

158 Rhodes, Mandy, 'Jack McConnell and Jim Wallace discuss twenty years of the Scottish Parliament', *Holyrood Magazine*, 22 May 2019

159 Stewart, Donald, *A Scot in Westminster*, The Catalone Press 1994

160 Ewing, Winnie, *Stop the World: The Autobiography of Winnie Ewing*, Birlinn, 2004

161 MacCormick, John, *The Flag in the Wind*, Birlinn, 2008

162 Twitter, @WelshGovernment, 4 January 2021

163 Fraser, Douglas, 'Scotland "Frozen Out" of Brussels', *The Herald*, 22 January 2007

164 Pasha-Robinson, Lucy, 'Anti-EU Ministers Show "Invincible Ignorance" Over European Court Says Top Ex-judge', *The Independent*, 22 April 2017

165 Rankin, Jennifer and Watson, Jim, 'How Boris Johnson's Brussels-Bashing Stories Shaped British Politics', *The Guardian*, 14 July 2019

166 See Prime Minister's statement to the House of Commons, Hansard, 3 February 2020

167 'How Ireland Gets Its Way: An Unlikely Diplomatic Superpower', *The Economist*, 17 July 2020

168 McEwen, Nicola, et al., 'Intergovernmental Relations in the UK: Time for a Radical Overhaul?', *Political Quarterly*, 14 June 2020

169 ibid.

170 'Penny Mourdant: The UK Can't Veto Turkey Joining the EU', BBC News, 22 May 2016

171 Healey, Derek, 'Sir John Curtice: Why a Westminster Win Could See SNP Declare Independence', *The Courier*, 17 September 2020

172 '92% Believe Ireland Should Remain in the EU', *Irish Examiner*, 8 May 2018

173 Sturgeon, Nicola, speech to Foreign Affairs Committee of the French National Assembly, 19 February 2019 – www.gov.scot/publications/first-ministers-speech-at-french-national-assembly/

174 Salmond, Alex, speech to Brookings Institute, 9 April 2013 – www.brookings.edu/wp-content/uploads/2013/03/20130409_scotland_salmond_transcript.pdf

175 'Brexit Vote: Nicola Sturgeon Statement in Full', BBC News, 24 June 2016

176 Sturgeon, Nicola, speech to Arctic Circle Assembly, 7 October 2016 – www.gov.scot/publications/arctic-circle-assembly-2016-fm-speech/

177 Scottish Government, *UK internal market: initial assessment of UK Government proposals*, 12 August 2020

178 McEwen, Nicola, et al., 'Intergovernmental Relations in the UK: Time for a Radical Overhaul?', *Political Quarterly*, 14 June 2020

179 Salamone, Anthony, *Scotland and the Spirit of Europe – Protecting Scotland's European Relations in the Face of Brexit*, European Merchants Edinburgh Ltd., 30 November 2019

180 Andrews, Kieran, 'Independent Scotland Would Find it Hard Work to Re-join Says Merkel Ally', *The Press and Journal*, 17 February 2017

181 Kirby, Will, 'Brussels Bigwig Claims Crumbling EU "Cannot Afford" to Lose Scotland as Brexit Talks Loom', *Daily Express*, 15 February 2017

182 *Reuters*, 26 June 2016

183 'German Minister backs Sturgeon as "strong political leader"', *Scotland on Sunday*, 19 March 2017

184 Andrew Marr programme, BBC One, 2 February 2020

185 Farand, Chloe, 'Spain Gives Up Threat to Veto Independent Scotland's Application to Re-join the EU', *The Independent*, 2 April 2017

186 'Spain Would Not Oppose Future Independent Scotland Re-joining EU', *Reuters*, 20 November 2018

187 TD stands for Teachta Dála, deputy to the Dáil

188 'Ireland Should Help "Fast-track" Scotland Back into the EU', *The Scotsman*, 26 June 2016

189 Visit Brussels website – https://visit.brussels/site/binaries/content/assets/pdf/figures_en_1.pdf

190 Channel 4 News, 4 September 2019

191 Salamone, Anthony, report to Europe Committee, *Scotland's Engagement with the European Union – Insights from Third Countries and Regions*, October 2019 on behalf of the Scottish Centre on European Relations

192 Kahn, Mehreen, 'New Hanseatic States Stick Together in EU Big League', *Financial Times*, 27 November 2018 & 'Northern Member States Unite on Eurozone Reform', *The Economist*, 8 December 2018

193 Hughes, Kirsty, 'Scotland's Borders and Independence', *Sceptical Scot*, 16 August 2020

194 'Henry McLeish: Scotland Needs to Bypass UK on Brexit', *The National*, 4 June 2020

195 Heather, Alastair, 'Why Finns believe Scotland could become Nordic nation Number 6', *The Scotsman*, 17 May 2020

196 Levin, Dan, 'In the Battle for Sovereignty of a Disputed Arctic Island, Canada and Denmark Use Whisky and Schnapps', *The New York Times*, 7 November 2016

197 'Taoiseach Stresses Desire Not to Fall Out With Scotland Over Rockall', *Irish Times*, 28 June 2019

198 Muller Stuart, Mark, 'Using Culture and Scotland's Soft Power to Help to Resolve Conflict', speech to the Royal Society of Arts, 24 November 2017

199 'Why Bjork May Really be a Scot', *Daily Telegraph*, 3 March 2001

200 Horne, Mark, 'Expert Argues Vikings Carried Redhead Gene to Scotland', *The Scotsman*, 24 November 2013

201 'Sweden Welcomes Scotland's "No" Vote', *The Local*, 19 September 2014

202 Nordic Council press release, 'Scottish Parliament Seeks Closer Cooperation With the Nordic Council', 30 January 2020

203 The islands represented one of the few success stories of the League of Nations and has maintained a special status. For further information see – www.um.fi/the-special-status-of-the-aland-islands

204 Dreyer, Bjarke S, *Dear Scotland you'd be very welcome to join the Nordic Council*, 2 February 2020

205 Heather, Alastair, 'Why Finns believe Scotland could become Nordic nation Number 6', *The Scotsman*, 17 May 2020

206 Defence Select Committee Report, *On Thin Ice: UK Defence in the Arctic*, 15 August 2018

207 Robertson, Angus, 'High Time to Join Our Friends in the North and Face the Arctic Challenge', *The Scotsman*, 29 November 2011

208 Scottish Government, *Arctic Connections: Scotland's Arctic Policy Framework*, 23 September 2019

209 Bailes, Alyson, *The Faroe Islands and the Arctic: Messages for Scotland*, Scottish Global Forum, 3 December 2013

210 Depledge, Duncan and Dodds, Klaus, *The United Kingdom, Scotland and the Arctic*, Arctic Institute, 5 December 2017

211 For more information see – www.arcticcircle.org

212 Bailes, Alyson, *Scotland's External Relations: Is There Life after 'No'?*, Scottish Global Forum

213 Tømmerbakke, Siri Gulliksen, 'Scotland Wants to Become the European Gateway to the Arctic', *High North News*, 24 September 2019

214 '*Borgen* Star Sidse Knudsen Says She Feels at "Home" in Scotland', *Deadline News*, 3 February 2013

215 Dinwoodie, Robbie, 'Salmond Defiant in His Defence of "Arc of Insolvency", *The Herald*, 15 October 2008

216 Fine Gael press release, 5 January 2020

217 *All Points North – Scottish Government Nordic Baltic Policy Statement*, 27 September 2017

218 'Putin Before Vote Says He'd Reverse Soviet Collapse If He Could', *Reuters*, 2 March 2018

219 McGuiness, Damien, 'How a Cyber Attack Transformed Estonia', BBC News, 27 April 2017

220 Amnesty International, *Russia Country Report – Everything you need to know about human rights in Russia*

221 'Scottish Independence: Icelandic President Olafur Grimsson Enters Debate', BBC News, 15 December 2012

222 Norwegian Ministry of Foreign Affairs press release, 30 June 2020

223 'Peace-building as Small State Foreign Policy: Norway's Peace Engagement in a Changing International Context' in *International Studies* 49(3&4), SAGE Publications, 2014, pp. 207–231

224 MacCormick v. Lord Advocate (1953) SC 396 – Court of Session (on appeal)

225 Atkins, Ros, BBC News, 9 December 2020. See also Twitter, @BBCRosAtkins, 9 December 2020

226 Wintour, Patrick, 'Bush largely ignored UK advice on postwar Iraq, Chilcot Inquiry finds', *Guardian*, 6 July 2016

227 House of Commons Foreign Affairs Committee, *Libya: Examination of intervention and collapse and the UK's future policy options*, Third Report of Session 2016–17

228 House of Commons Foreign Affairs Committee, *Extension of Offensive British Military Operations to Syria*, Second Report of Session 2015–16

229 'Syria Crisis: Cameron Loses Commons Vote on Syria Action', BBC News, 30 August 2013

230 House of Commons, 17 March 2003

231 O'Sullivan, Kevin, 'John Bercow: Brexit is the Most Colossal Foreign Policy Blunder in the Post-war Period', *Irish Times*, 15 January 2020

232 MacShne, Denis, *Brexit and the decline of British Foreign Policy,* Carnegie Europe, 28 July 2017

233 Henley, John, 'A Shambles on Which the Sun Never Sets: How the World Sees Brexit', *The Guardian* 6 April 2019

234 House of Commons Foreign Affairs Committee, *Global Britain*, Sixth Report of the Session 2017–19.

235 I never have liked the term small country to describe Scotland given that in European and world terms it is a middle or normal sized country. At time of writing the National Records of Scotland put the population at 5,463,000 which is about the same size as Denmark, Norway and Finland and placed about 118 out of 235 according to United Nations Population Division estimates (www.worldometers.info/world-population/population-by-country/) so pretty much bang in the middle.

236 White Paper, *Scotland's Future – Your Guide to an Independent Scotland,* Scottish Government, November 2013, Chapter 7, pp. 224–25

237 Dáil Éireann debate, 28 June 1963 – www.oireachtas.ie/en/debates/debate/dail/1963-06-28/2/

238 'How This Hotel in the Highlands Could End a Bloodbath in the Caucasus', *The Herald*, 13 December 2003

239 Beyond Borders Scotland – www.beyondbordersscotland.com

240 Section 105, House of Commons Foreign Affairs Committee, *Libya: Examination of intervention and collapse and the UK's future policy options*, Third Report of Session 2016–17

241 Siegel, Robert, 'Powell's Cautions on Iraq', *NPR*, 20 April 2004

242 Muller Stuart, Mark, 'Using Culture and Scotland's Soft Power to Help to Resolve Conflict', speech to the Royal Society of Arts, 24 November 2017

243 Pratt, David, 'UN's Top Diplomat: Scotland is Perfect Setting for Syrian Peace Initiative', *The Herald*, 15 May 2016

244 Scottish Government press release, 'Scotland Supports Syrian Peace Process', 7 May 2016

245 Women's role in conflict resolution: First Minister's UN speech (05/07/2017) – www.gov.scot/publications/womens-role-in-conflict-resolution-fm-un-speech/

246 Muller Stuart, Mark, *Storm in the Desert: Britain's Intervention in Libya and the Arab Spring'*, Birlinn, 2017

247 Muller Stuart, Mark, 'Using Culture and Scotland's Soft Power to Help to Resolve Conflict', speech to the Royal Society of Arts, 24 November 2017

248 Mbeki, Thabo, speech, 'Address at the Scottish Parliament, 13 June 2001', South African History Online – sahistory.org.za

249 Salamone, Anthony, report to Europe Committee, *Scotland's Engagement with the European Union – Insights from Third Countries and Regions*, October 2019 on behalf of the Scottish Centre on European Relations

250 'Johnson "refused to give Sturgeon climate summit role"', BBC News, 4 February 2020

251 Duncan, Alan, Foreign Office Minister, House of Commons, 3 December 2018

252 'Nicola Sturgeon recognised by UN for advancing gender equality', *The Scotsman*, 6 February 2019

253 First Minister's UN speech, 5 July 2017 – www.gov.scot/publications/womens-role-in-conflict-resolution-fm-un-speech/

254 Müller, Klaus Peter, 'The Referendum in Austrian, German and Swiss Media', in Blain, Neil and Hutchison, David with Hassan, Gerry, *Scotland's Referendum and the Media: National and International Perspectives*, Edinburgh University Press 2016

255 Brookings Institute, 9 April 2013

256 Scottish Government publications, *The Scottish Diaspora and Diaspora Strategy: Insights and Lessons from Ireland*, 29 May 2009

257 UK in a Changing Europe, Brexit Witness Archive – www.ukandeu.ac.uk/brexit-witness-archive

258 Boffey, Daniel, 'Confidence in UK's Global Role Plunges After Brexit, Poll Finds', *The Guardian*, 28 September 2020

259 Foreign Affairs Committee Session, 10 January 2013

260 Anholt-Gfk, Roper Nations Brands Index SM: 2018 report for Scotland, 22 January 2019 –www.gov.scot/publications/anholt-gfk-roper-nation-brands-indexsm-2018-report-scotland/pages/4/

261 Hansard, House of Commons, 3 December 2018

262 Pratt, David, 'Scotland's Foreign Policy: How Should We Interact With the World', *The National*, 30 November 2018

263 See endnote 104

264 Brzozowski, Alexandra, 'Walloonia Threatens to Veto Brexit Deal', *Euractiv*, 11 December 2020

265 McClory, Jonathan, *Gauging International Perceptions: Scotland and Soft Power*, British Council Scotland, 2020

266 Institute for Government, interview with Jack McConnell, 6 September 2018 – www.instituteforgovernment.org.uk/ministers-reflect/person/lord-mcconnell/

267 McClory, Jonathan, *Gauging International Perceptions: Scotland and Soft Power*, British Council Scotland, 2020

268 Brocklehurst, Steven, 'Why Did Nelson Mandela Thank Glasgow', BBC News, 9 October 2018

269 Muller Stuart, Mark, 'Using Culture and Scotland's Soft Power to Help to Resolve Conflict', speech to the Royal Society of Arts, 24 November 2017

270 'How Pub Sing Songs and Bono Brought Ireland to a Seat at the Highest Table', *Irish Times*, 23 June 2020,

271 Docherty-Hughes, Martin, 'Scottish Independence: If Ireland and Norway Can Win Election to the UN Security Council, We Could Too', *The Scotsman*, 23 June 2020

272 Baillie, Sasha, *The Seat of European Institutions: An example of small state Influence in European Decision Making*, European University Institute, 1996

273 Coveney, Simon, statement, 17 June 2020 (as viewed on *RTE*)

274 Lithuanian Foreign Minister speech to Heads of Missions, 3 July 2018 – Speech by Minister Linas Linkevičius at the Annual Meeting of Heads of Diplomatic Missions of the Republic of Lithuania, Ministry of Foreign Affairs (urm.lt)

275 Jackson, Ben, *The Case for Scottish Independence: A History of Nationalist Political Thought in Modern Scotland*, Cambridge University Press, 2020

276 Sturgeon, Nicola, speech at University of Georgetown, 5 February 2019 – www.snp.org/first-minister-nicola-sturgeons-speech-at-georgetown-university/

277 Bailes, Alyson, 'Scotland's External Relations: Is There Life after "No"?', *Sunday Herald*

Luath Press Limited

committed to publishing well written books worth reading

LUATH PRESS takes its name from Robert Burns, whose little collie Luath (*Gael.*, swift or nimble) tripped up Jean Armour at a wedding and gave him the chance to speak to the woman who was to be his wife and the abiding love of his life. Burns called one of the 'Twa Dogs' Luath after Cuchullin's hunting dog in Ossian's *Fingal*. Luath Press was established in 1981 in the heart of Burns country, and is now based a few steps up the road from Burns' first lodgings on Edinburgh's Royal Mile. Luath offers you distinctive writing with a hint of unexpected pleasures.

Most bookshops in the UK, the US, Canada, Australia, New Zealand and parts of Europe, either carry our books in stock or can order them for you. To order direct from us, please send a £sterling cheque, postal order, international money order or your credit card details (number, address of cardholder and expiry date) to us at the address below. Please add post and packing as follows: UK – £1.00 per delivery address; overseas surface mail – £2.50 per delivery address; overseas airmail – £3.50 for the first book to each delivery address, plus £1.00 for each additional book by airmail to the same address. If your order is a gift, we will happily enclose your card or message at no extra charge.

Luath Press Limited
543/2 Castlehill
The Royal Mile
Edinburgh EH1 2ND
Scotland
Telephone: +44 (0)131 225 4326 (24 hours)
Email: sales@luath. co.uk
Website: www.luath.co.uk